Modelling
Toy Soldiers

JOHN PAXTON SHERIFF

Modelling
Toy Soldiers

JOHN PAXTON SHERIFF

ROBERT HALE · LONDON

Photoset in North Wales by
Derek Doyle & Associates, Mold, Clwyd.
Printed in Great Britain by
St Edmundsbury Press Ltd, Bury St Edmunds, Suffolk.
Bound by WBC Book Manufacturers Limited,
Bridgend, Mid-Glamorgan.

Contents

Illustrations

· ILLUSTRATIONS ·

ILLUSTRATION CREDITS

Poste Militaire Promotions: 24. Trophy Miniatures Wales Ltd: 29. Alec Tiranti Ltd: 31. All other illustrations are from the author's collection.

ACKNOWLEDGEMENT

The author would like to thank Cassell plc for permission to use the quote on page 27, taken from *Uniforms of the American Revolution* by John Mollo and Malcolm McGregor.

Introduction

The title of this book – *Modelling Toy Soldiers* – can both inspire and daunt a newcomer to the subject. Those three words make what at first glance seems a complicated process sound simple when, as most people realize, any task becomes simple only when the required skills have been learnt.

Some basic skills are needed, of course, and those people who are all thumbs when attempting intricate manual work will always find miniature modelling difficult. But the degree of skill required to produce a model of the human form depends on the intended sophistication of the sculpture – on how closely the finished work is expected to match or mimic real life. To produce a sculpture equivalent to Michelangelo's *David* requires genius; to make an acceptable garden gnome requires talents of a much lower order.

Models of soldiers have always been popular. They cover all periods of history, have been made from an astonishing variety of materials, and come in all shapes and sizes. They range from the incredible, lifesize terracotta armies discovered in Xi'an, China, to the 190,000 tiny figures massed on Captain William Siborne's 18-foot-wide diorama of the Battle of Waterloo, first displayed in London in 1938. The figures were too small to have any detail, yet viewed *en masse* those British, Prussian and French armies were a magnificent sight. Those last few words catch the essential attraction and charm of toy soldiers. The undoubted crudeness, lack of detail and poor paintwork on many of the figures produced is of no concern; they are meant to be viewed not individually, but as part of a group.

The world of model soldiers can be split into two distinct classes: connoisseur figures and toy soldiers. Connoisseur figures come in many sizes, but commonly stand to a height of 54 mm, 75 mm, and the currently popular 120 mm. They are highly detailed, are often mounted on ornamental bases and they are meant to stand alone. Toy soldiers – certainly in the UK – have for many years been manufactured to a standard 54 mm, and are usually available in boxed sets.

This concept of sets, and massed displays, is one of the main reasons why collectors of toy soldiers might decide to produce their own figures. Toy soldiers manufactured in tin alloy – the standard material – have long outgrown their 'toy' image, and as a consequence have acquired prices that reflect their collectibility and appreciating value. So collectors who want to create, for example, a display of the Trooping the Colour, would need to locate the exact figures they need for the regiments involved (and that can take time), then spend a great deal of money. The alternative is highly appealing: producing your own toy soldiers means that you get exactly the right figures, when you want them – and at a fraction of the cost. Colourful displays can be produced for your own pleasure or, as in Captain Siborne's case, to recreate in exhibition a particular battle or event for the general public.

But whatever your intentions, the aim of this book is to guide you through the production of a toy soldier, from its conception in the mind's eye to the resplendent, uniformed figure painted in shiny enamels. From there you can happily embark on a limited form of mass production that can lead to the build-up of highly impressive displays or, if desired, mass production on a grand scale and the establishment of a satisfactory small business.

1 Creating a Basic Master Figure

We've already seen that toy soldiers are meant to be viewed not on their own but in small or large groups. So when we set out to make our first, single toy soldier, it makes sense if we build into the initial modelling process a method of reproducing that figure – or others like it – again and again.

Most sculptors begin with an armature, a skeleton of wire or other suitable material that is correctly proportioned and stiff enough to hold the soft modelling materials in position. The design and production of a simple one that suits our purpose will be our first task. But instead of building a fresh armature each time we embark on a new figure, it is much easier to produce from that first armature a crude master figure which can easily be replicated (see Chapter 4). Then, when we go to our work bench to begin our next figure, instead of starting from scratch all we need do is take one of our naked master figures, bend head, body and limbs into the required pose, and use modelling materials to build up details of the uniform that accurately portrays the period and regiment.

To avoid confusion between this basic master figure and the detailed master figures that are the models for finished toy soldiers, I will henceforth refer to the basic master figure as Minikin.

In this chapter we will look at:

- the simple master figure
- basic human anatomy and proportion
- making an armature
- creating the Minikin

Let's begin by clarifying this concept of a master figure.

A rank of toy soldiers will have a number of figures similarly posed: standing to attention, with rifles at the aim, or perhaps marching with weapons at the slope. Every figure we model will need to be replicated a number of times. So from our first *finished* toy soldier – painstakingly modelled from a variety of malleable materials that are all too easily damaged – it is wise to make a silicone rubber mould and produce a durable casting in tin alloy that faithfully reproduces every detail of our finished model. This becomes our master figure. Because the mould will be used to cast dozens of clones, it will eventually become damaged, or wear out. When it does, a replacement mould will be made from the metal master figure, not from the original (which, if it was made from a non-hardening modelling compound, may no longer exist).

The Minikin dealt with in this chapter can also be reproduced by casting from a mould, but its basic form is arrived at reasonably quickly before any serious modelling is started. It is an intermediary in the sense that it comes between the wire structure known as the armature (which it replaces) and the completed figure, and it is a convenience because it saves time; the tedious groundwork has been done and each time we start a new model we can move straight to the serious modelling and sculpting without having to worry about size, or proportion (although as we work we will still need to keep checking measurements).

From the above it will be seen that a sculptor's basic wire armature needs to be made only rarely. But because the Minikin that replaces it becomes the foundation for all that follows, it must be accurately proportioned despite its simplicity. And to achieve that, we need to know some simple facts about human anatomy.

The Simple Master Figure

When anyone first sets out to create a very small model of the human figure, a number of common errors are made. The head is almost always too big, the arms are too long, the legs are too short and the feet and hands are too big. Making a model with the correct proportions cannot be done 'by eye' alone. It is achieved by the use of calipers or dividers, and – until the details

Basic Human Anatomy and Proportion

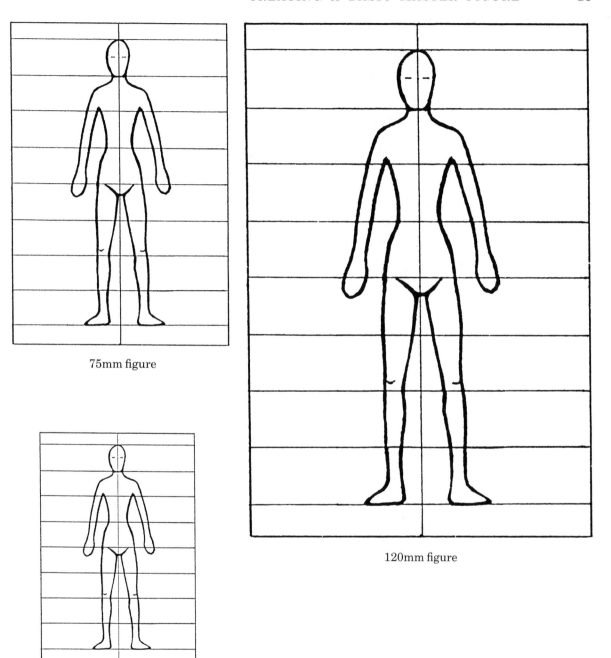

75mm figure

54mm figure

120mm figure

A basic anatomy diagram, with the figure divided into eight units

are memorized – continual reference to a diagram.

The easiest way of calculating proportion is to begin with a basic unit of measurement which can be used for comparison. In the case of the human figure this is usually the head and, as a rough and ready guide, we can begin by saying that the complete human form measures about eight heads. If we take our standard 54 mm toy soldier, that means that its head – one eighth of its full height – will measure approximately 6.75 mm.

The hip joint is the body's mid-point. The measurements from there to the top of the skull, and to the heel when the leg is extended, are the same – in the case of our 54 mm toy soldier, about 27 mm. It's important to remember that when we say the legs are equal in length to the torso and head combined, we mean from that all-important hip joint. It's all too easy to memorize the rule, but mistakenly assume that legs are measured from where they fork.

The navel, which in a clothed figure can conveniently be thought of as the waistline, is some five heads from the base of the heel: about 34 mm. A hand is approximately one-tenth the length of the whole figure (5.4 mm), the foot – in a male – about one-sixth (9 mm). Both are about the same width at their widest point. On soldiers standing to attention with arms straight and fingers curled, the position of the knuckles is almost exactly 3½ heads up from the base of the heel: about 23.5 mm. Finally, one other measurement which always needs to be accurate on figures wearing tight breeches or leggings is the position of the knee. This comes slightly above the halfway point between hip and heel: just over 15 mm.

Making an Armature

An armature is a skeleton made from wire that is pliable enough to be shaped by fingers or pliers, but stiff enough to retain its shape when being covered with a modelling material. If you ever made a drawing of a stick man when you were a child, you will know exactly what an armature looks like. Suitable thin wire can be obtained from hardware stores, or from gardening centres – especially those with a department devoted to Bonsai. Think of the size of a toy soldier, and buy wire that is the right thickness for a tiny skeleton, malleable enough to work with but firm enough to hold its shape.

When you start work you will need three pieces. To begin with simply cut them to a length convenient to handle – say, 143 mm.

One piece will act as your model's backbone, stretching from the groin to the top of the head. Take this 143 mm length of wire, hold it vertically, and lay a second piece horizontally across it for

Needle-nosed pliers, soft aluminium wire and ordinary thread – all you need for making a simple armature

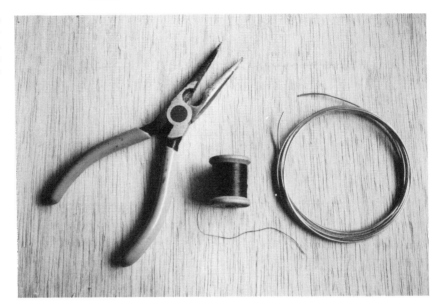

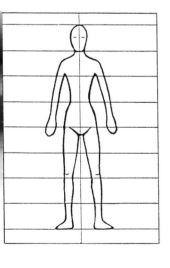

the shoulders and arms. A good position is about 25 mm down from the top. This wire should be fixed in position by twisting or winding the two wires together, and you should finish up with a little less than 75 mm sticking out on either side of the central column.

Now you must begin thinking about accurate measurements. Because this is the skeleton around which your soldier will be modelled, you must make sure that your work is a little under-size. Consult your anatomy diagram, see how far down the spinal column the hips should be in relation to the shoulders on a correctly proportioned figure, and subtract about a millimetre from this measurement before twisting the wire firmly in place. Again, you will be left with about 75 mm on either side.

Your next concern is the width of the shoulders. The wire to form these is already in position across the spinal column, and it must now be bent down on both sides to make the arms. From the diagram of the human form you know that the average man's shoulders are fractionally over two heads wide – about 14 mm. So, still working a little under-size, bend each arm down so that the shoulders are about 13 mm wide.

In the same way, go to the second piece of wire you fixed in position at hip level, and bend each side down to form your skeleton's legs. Remember that on a male figure the hips are always narrower than the shoulders, so they will be less than 13 mm wide – 10 mm or 11 mm is about right.

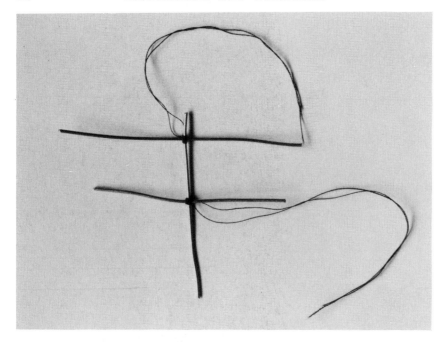

Two pieces of wire have been laid across a third, and tied with thread. The central piece will be cut to size, the other two bent down to form the arms and legs

The finished armature should have the arms straight, and held slightly away from where the body will be; the legs should also be straight and slightly apart.

Working on a 54 mm armature can be very fiddly. Twisting the wires to hold them in position doesn't always work, so another good method is to bind them in place with cotton. The cotton can always be made into a strong fixture by soaking it with a suitable glue when you are sure the cross wires are correctly positioned. Alternatively, you can make sure the joins are absolutely permanent by squeezing blobs of Milliput (see Chapter 2) around them and letting them harden.

You now have two options. The armature you are making is to be used as the frame for the Minikin. You can proceed by snipping off the excess wire so that the arms and legs are a little shorter than they will be on your master figure. Or you can leave them – and the untrimmed spinal column that still extends beyond the head and groin – as they are, cutting them to size only when you have successfully created the Minikin. I favour the latter course. Toy soldiers are always awkward to handle, and having convenient bits sticking out here and there always comes in handy. Also, the pieces of wire projecting downwards can be used at a later stage to secure the basic master figure in its mould box.

Some firms selling modelling materials supply handy plastic

armatures, either singly or in packs. Unfortunately, most of these are in the larger sizes. Alec Tiranti of Theale, Reading, stocks 110 mm versions.

Creating the Minikin

Readers of this book will have different ideas about the way they want to tackle modelling toy soldiers. I have already mentioned making a Minikin that can be reproduced in the form of a casting from a silicone rubber mould and thus used over and over again. But not all of you will want to do that. Some of you will be planning to model every one of your toy soldiers from an armature outwards, every time, leaving the duplication that requires some messing about with hot metal to more adventurous souls.

In either case – making a Minikin to be reproduced, or as the first stage of every single figure – the procedure is virtually the same. The only difference is that if you intend making all your figures by hand then the course of action discussed here is not a stage with a clearly defined conclusion – the Minikin – but the gradual, continuous build-up of your first figure from the armature outwards.

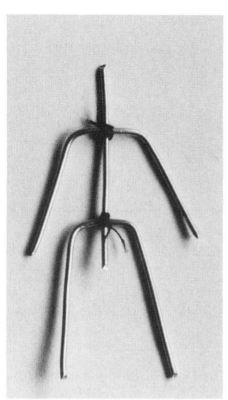

The completed armature. The tied sections can be made firmer in a number of ways – for example by the application of glue, or Milliput

Modelling materials are dealt with in detail in Chapter 2, but my suggestion now is for you to make your first Minikin from Plasticine, which always stays malleable, or Fimo, which is handled in much the same way but gradually hardens. Plasticine is very easy to work with, but warm hands tend to make it too soft; that can be cured by placing the material in the fridge for a few minutes while you take a coffee break. Fimo is, in my opinion, a little more difficult to work with. It feels slightly 'springy' to the touch, and when it does harden it has a tendency to expand slightly. There are other materials that go by different brand names, and it might be a good idea to try several, then stick to the one that suits your modelling style.

For most of the work the only tools you will need are a craft knife, a small pair of sharp-nosed pliers and your fingers. You will find a small shaping tool is useful when you are working in the vees where the arms and legs join the trunk, and when shaping the head and neck.

The procedure is to create a recognizable human shape by using your chosen material to add thickness to your armature. Initially there's no need to worry about measurements. Arms and legs will develop into long, thin lengths like macaroni. The body will have more bulk, and there will be a very small cylinder for the neck. Try to work so that the wire of your armature is embedded in the centre of the trunk and each limb. As you progress you will soon discover that, when working with either of the recommended materials, the lengths of wire extending through the arms and legs make the embryo model easy to handle.

When the Minikin has begun to take shape and you need to refer to measurements, once again work very slightly under-size. Remember that if you are modelling the Minikin for duplication you are doing it for future convenience. In order to save unnecessary work during later stages it needs to be reasonably close to the right bulk, but still slim enough to enable you to add a uniform – jacket, trousers, boots. Don't be afraid to adjust the shape and size of your armature while you are working. If you find that adding modelling material means that the shoulders will be much too wide, reduce their width by bending the armature. Do the same when other measurements go wrong, and if you get in a complete mess, scrape off all the modelling material and start again.

The main measurements from which all others are determined are the overall length from the base of the heel to the crown of the head, and the size of the head itself. When you have built up the body and limbs, make an egg-shaped blob for the head and slide it onto the armature wire sticking out of the small, cylindrical neck. Refer to the anatomy diagram and use your calipers and small shaping tool to make the head the correct length from chin to crown, and to ensure that the head is in the correct position in relation to the shoulders – these slope, of course, and you will see that the chin is just over half a head above their lowest point.

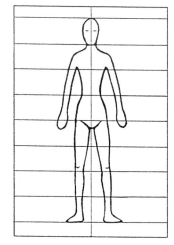

You can now establish the height of your toy soldier (54 mm) by cutting the legs to the correct length. If you have previously snipped the wire short this will simply mean removing excess modelling material from their ends. A quick check with dividers should ensure that not only is the overall length of the figure correct, but that the other important measurement – from the hip joint – is the same (27 mm) in both directions.

The length of the arms is adjusted in the same way, remembering that the measurement is to the tips of the extended fingers (just over three heads from the heel). It's a good idea to make a crude hand, so use your own finger and thumb to squeeze a little flat portion of the right length at the end of each arm.

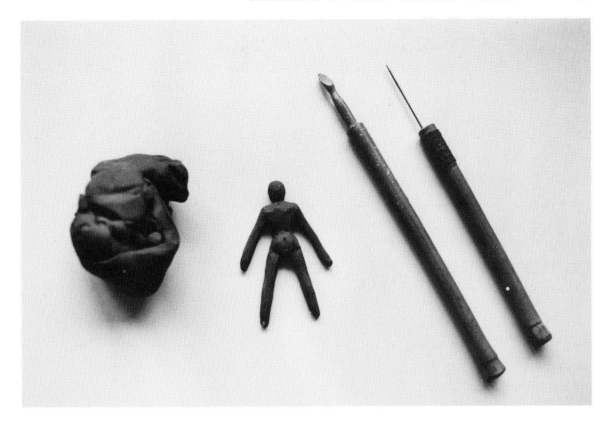

The completed Minikin, made by covering the wire armature with Plasticine which is then cut and moulded to shape. Constant reference must be made to the anatomy diagram

All that remains is to give the tiny Minikin another careful examination, checking head size and its position in relation to the shoulders, shoulder width, arm and leg lengths, and general overall appearance. It's not a bad idea to give the completed figure a couple of blobs for feet, flattened under the soles.

Modellers with different methods may now part company. The person who intends to reproduce the Minikin might decide to move on to Chapter 4, there to learn all about mould-making. The modeller who has decided to work straight through to the completed toy soldier can simply advance to Chapter 2.

2 The Toy Soldier: Preliminary Work

The individual toy soldier can be made from any good modelling material, and one will generally choose the material used to construct the Minikin of Chapter 1. At this stage the only way modellers may differ in their way of working is that some will continue building on the original Minikin they created, while those who jumped to Chapter 4 may by now have done some casting; they will go to their box of gleaming tin-alloy Minikins and select one to use as a foundation.

Whichever route you choose, by the end of this and the next chapter you will have modelled your very first toy soldier – and you will again arrive at an intriguing fork in the road. But first there is some preliminary work to do, and in this chapter we will be looking at:

- materials
- tools
- choosing an era, regiment and pose
- how much detail?
- research

Materials

Delightful toy soldiers have been made from paper cut to shape, from papier mâché shaped over a wire frame, from plaster of

Paris poured into crude moulds. They have been carved out of wax, soapstone, wood or ivory, and modelled in natural clay and dozens of man-made compounds such as two-part epoxy resins or putties that set like concrete, or others that, like the ubiquitous Plasticine, never set at all and tend to droop when warm.

There is no ideal, though some materials are fiendishly difficult to work with while others result in a flimsy figure with no bulk. For that reason paper can be ruled out at once for our purpose (though it can be very useful for accessories such as shields, flags and pennants). Plaster of Paris needs a mould from the start, so is of no use at all. Soapstone, wood or ivory are good materials from which to carve a complete figure, but clearly useless as a modelling material to be added to a basic figure. Wax can be bought in blocks from good model or craft shops, is a delight to work with, moulds or carves easily and allows for fine detail. Unfortunately, it won't (as far as I am aware) stick to anything except wax.

You have already made your Minikin. If you decided to avoid casting you will have before you a figure made from Plasticine or Fimo, or something very similar. My advice is to continue with those materials. Many of my early soldiers were made completely of Plasticine, and when used to make a 54 mm figure its advantages, in my opinion, far outweigh any faults. If used to make a large figure without an armature it tends to 'sink', resulting in a figure with short legs; but you will be adding it to a diminutive, solid form, and that works well. Yes, it does become too soft when warm, but ten minutes' rest solves that problem and anyone who remembers playing with Plasticine will know that it is easily rolled into threads as thin as vermicelli (when flattened they make ideal belts), and the tiniest pieces (noses, ears, buttons) can be stuck securely to the main form without any visible join.

If you chose the casting route which produced a number of Minikins, from now on you will be working with a metal figure. The immediate advantage is that you have something solid to get hold of. Again, that figure has to be built up, and you must choose a modelling material that will adhere to your metal Minikin. This is partly good news, partly bad. You have a much wider selection to choose from, most set hard and result in a very durable figure that will stand rough handling – but almost without exception they are more difficult to work with than Plasticine.

The compound which has become the favourite of many military modellers is Milliput, a two-part epoxy putty that comes in grades such as standard, superfine white, and silver grey. In appearance the standard form is like two rolls of green or yellow Plasticine, but when equal amounts are kneaded together – in just the same way balls of different-coloured Plasticine are combined to form a ball of another colour – the result is a malleable compound that hardens very gradually (in a room of average temperature you will have about four hours before the compound becomes too hard to work). Milliput will stick to itself or metal, and can be rolled into threads, strips or sheets. When still soft, fine details such as buttons and buckles can be shaped with an artist's brush dipped in water; when almost hard, strips can be cut like pastry to form perfect belts; when completely set or cured it can be sawn, sanded or drilled.

Other similar products include Kneadatite and Sylmasta (only recently available in this country). The latter 'sets like stone' and is ideal for making master figures. Several of the inexpensive car body fillers available at any motor factors are ideal for building up bulky helmets, packs or pouches. Plastic Padding is just one I have used.

In the early stages of modelling you are unlikely to need glue, but when your soldier is nearing completion there will be weapons, swords, muskets and other bits and bobs to attach. Modern glues are excellent, and the instant superglues appear to be the most suitable for this kind of miniature modelling. But it has been suggested that the lead present in most tin alloys gradually breaks down their adhesion, and for that reason I have always used Araldite Rapid.

Tools

Most hobbies can be enjoyed just as much with a few basic hand tools as they can with a room full of expensive equipment that frightens the neighbours and drains the national grid. Modelling toy soldiers is no exception, and the two most necessary basics are not even tools at all. They are a good work surface, and an adjustable light.

You will recall that in Chapter 1 I talked about a 54 mm soldier having a head measuring 6.75 mm. It is literally a small step from there to a nose less than 2 mm long, and eyes – well, the eyes really don't bear thinking about (in toy soldiers anyway they're usually just painted dots). But you can see why a light that is bright and can be moved so that the illumination falls exactly where it's needed is probably your number one priority.

A sheet of thick plywood makes a good work surface. You will be doing a lot of cutting with sharp knives and a certain amount of drilling, and some of the compounds like Milliput are best

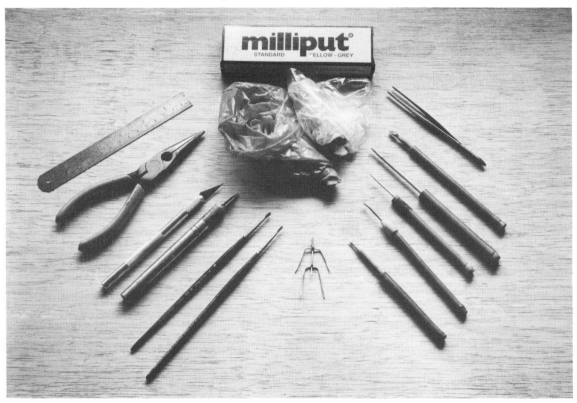

The completed armature, a box of Milliput, and a selection of tools suitable for detailed modelling. Most of those on the right are home-made

kept off polished surfaces. It's a good idea to put a raised beading around three sides of your work surface, so that metal shavings and tiny balls of Plasticine and Milliput don't roll off the edges and get trodden into the carpet. You can also buy self-sealing cutting mats of non-glare polyvinyl, which heal themselves instantly after each cut.

Early modelling work will be done with your fingers. Once you get down to finer details you will need some modelling tools, and it's at this stage that you will begin to realize just how small toy soldiers are. Most small modelling tools are simply too clumsy. I made most of my own. One is simply a darning needle jammed into the end of a piece of bamboo, and you will soon find yourself doing similar improvising. Cocktail sticks are ideal. You can split a pencil, shape most of its length into a smooth handle (or wedge it into a short length of bamboo) and with coarse and fine sandpaper design a tip of the required shape. Do that several times and you will have a selection of tools suitable for specific tasks: flat ones for pressing around a soldier's waist to leave a narrow ridge (a waist belt); others with tips like tiny spatulas of different shapes with which you can form eye sockets, create folds in garments and shape a moustache.

For measuring you will need calipers or dividers, and a steel rule marked in millimetres.

A small vice is like an extra pair of hands (at a push you can put a soldier between the jaws of a heavy pair of pliers and hold them closed by stretching a strong elastic band around the hand grips). You will need a craft knife with assorted blades (some modellers use surgical scalpels), a mini saw, a soldering iron, a small pair of tweezers, needle and riffler files, and emery cloth and wet-and-dry papers for final smoothing. When working with Milliput, fine wire wool does that finishing job to perfection.

So far I haven't mentioned a magnifying glass. I have never needed one, but that is probably because I wear bi-focal spectacles – my own personal magnifiers. But, yes, I'm sure that most people setting out to model toy soldiers will need a magnifying glass for occasional use, and that brings me neatly to the range of tools that are helpful without being indispensable or even necessary.

Within this luxury range you will find magnifiers with a built-in daylight-simulation lamp, and headband magnifiers that leave both hands free. You may like the idea of a small turntable so that you can view your model from all sides, and if that kind of thing appeals to you there is a wonderful system called the Vice Squad, in which ELS 2009 is a small device that clamps to a workbench and through a system of arms and joints allows a model to be worked on from every angle, including upside down.

One final word on tools. There are several miniature power drills on the market. They often come with the chuck at the end of a flexible drive, and all have a range of tiny drill bits and milling cutters of various shapes that look very much like those used by a dentist. They are wonderful to use, and for some tasks this is one luxury tool that really is indispensable.

Choosing an Era, Regiment and Pose

When deciding on what your finished toy soldier is going to look like, begin with the panoramic view and move in gradually to the close-up. By this I mean that your first concern will be with an era, a particular and quite large slice of history. From your chosen era it is then a simple matter to zoom in and concentrate on one particular campaign – you will use that as your theme – and from that campaign choose a regiment that you know was involved. Your toy soldier will be a new recruit, and as your collection grows he will be joined by brothers in arms who will eventually march alongside other regiments.

The Minikin you have made is a tiny, anonymous figure that can nevertheless inspire an enormous amount of latent excitement. You can hold it in the palm of your hand and, in your imagination, clothe the slim form in garments ranging from the magnificent uniforms worn by the cavalry of the French First Empire to the drab khaki worn in the Ypres trenches. My guess is that when you decide on a uniform to model you will go for something colourful or showy, which means that if you are looking at British regiments your research will stop before you reach 1914.

Don't entirely rule out the less elaborate uniforms. One good reason for going for something more basic is that both the modelling and the painting will be less difficult. Although you will be working on just one figure, you must always remember that he is a toy soldier, and will be seen alongside usually five identical figures. So use your imagination to visualize the overall effect of that small group – a squad, or platoon, themselves part of the much larger regiment or battalion – and in doing so you will realize that even uniforms that are far from resplendent can look impressive when seen in neat ranks. What I am suggesting is that, despite your natural inclination, for a first toy soldier it might be wise to choose something relatively simple – and you can do so without in any way detracting from the appeal of the finished soldier.

Popular periods in military history include the English and American Civil Wars, the Jacobite Rebellions, the Napoleonic Wars and the Zulu Wars. There are, of course, many more, and within these and other periods you will find many reasonably plain uniforms. This is the panoramic view.

Let's say you decide to concentrate on the Napoleonic Wars, but rather than go for the Battle of Waterloo you opt for one of the battles of the Peninsular War. These include Vimiera, Talavera, Albuera, Vittoria and several others, and you would discover that many units took part in all battles. At Vittoria, for example, there were dozens of British line regiments – all known by their old numbers – plus units from the King's German Legion, the Portuguese division, and the Spanish infantry. The British light division included the 95th Rifles.

I mention them last because, having moved in from the panoramic view, I am now going to take a close look at a rifleman of that period, and use him as my basic model. He is an ideal choice. While his uniform has only two basic colours, green and black, and very little ornamentation, this rifleman is one of an exceedingly glamorous band of elite, skirmishing soldiers who look particularly attractive *en masse*.

It would be very impressive to have our soldier (and thus the group) with his musket at the aim – in either the kneeling or standing position. Unfortunately, this creates problems with modelling and casting, so for this first figure we will stand him at 'attention' and at the finishing stage place the musket in his right hand. Another good reason for choosing this pose is that it simplifies mould-making, as you will discover in Chapter 4.

One last point of interest before we move on. Completed toy soldiers can very easily be converted to represent other regiments, a task which often involves little more than the application of a different-coloured paint. By choosing a rifleman of the 95th we are providing ourselves with a basic figure which can be converted into a Portuguese rifleman of the 5th Cacadores, a soldier of the Portuguese 8th Infantry, a sharpshooter of the King's German Legion and an infantryman from any number of British line regiments of that period.

How Much Detail?

This would be a more valid question if we had chosen a hussar or carabinier as our first toy soldier, for their ornate uniforms would need to be drastically simplified for reproduction to be within the capabilities of an inexperienced modeller. As we have chosen a member of the 95th Rifles our problems are not so great, yet even so we must decide on the amount of detail we will include, and the way the detail we are going to incorporate is represented.

At its most intricate – and now I'm talking more about connoisseur figures than the humble toy soldier – every detail of the uniform would be carefully modelled. Jackets would have raised cuffs and lapels with clearly defined edges, ribbon and braid would stand proud, cap badges would be carefully detailed, and in each eye socket a tiny eyeball would rest between recognizable eyelids.

At the other end of the scale there is the toy soldier at its simplest. It will have shallow eye sockets, a rudimentary nose, virtually no raised details on the uniform apart from a crude belt and pouches, and everything else left to be represented at the painting stage – black dots for eyes, a painted moustache, chevrons, cap badge and so on.

As you can see from the above, the decision we have to make is split into two parts: how much detail – for in our model we can leave off packs and pouches and other accoutrements yet still have an authentic figure – and whether the detail we do include is to be modelled, or painted.

Research Military modellers have available to them hundreds of books on all aspects of warfare, and those concentrating on uniforms contain texts giving potted histories of regiments and the battles they fought, with detailed captions accompanying the colour plates with which all are copiously illustrated.

An example taken from *Uniforms of The American Revolution* by John Mollo and Malcolm McGregor goes like this:

Great Britain: Sergeant, Battalion Company, 1st Regiment of Foot Guards.

A 'Brigade' of foot guards, 1,000 strong, formed by selecting fifteen men from each of the sixty-four companies of the three regiments, was sent to America in 1776, where it was immediately formed into two battalions. An order of 12 March 1776 announced that:

His Majesty has been pleased to permit the officers of the detachment to make up an uniform with white lace like the privates of their respective regiments; the Sergeants to have their coats laced with white instead of gold ...

Officers and sergeants were also ordered to lay aside their spontoons and halberds and to arm themselves with fusils. The sergeant shown here is dressed in accordance with these orders, with the plain crimson waist-sash as worn by sergeants of the foot guards, and white lace formed into bastion loops, placed regularly, as on the dress of the privates of the regiment. The cartouche boxes of the foot guards were distinctive in that they had two brass buckles to which the belt was attached.

This wealth of detail (backed up by excellent colour plates) is still barely enough for the serious modeller who is – or should be – a stickler for authenticity. Having selected a soldier of the 95th Rifles as our first figure we are looking back to the period from 1808 to 1814. Even simple uniforms in those days were comparatively colourful and elaborate. Although we have chosen one of the least fussy it is nevertheless unfamiliar, and it's only when we set out to make a model that we realize just how much we need to know. Does our rifleman wear boots *and* gaiters? Are his trousers the same colour as his jacket? Does he have one row of buttons, or more – and how many are there? And what about his hairstyle; does he have a queue (pigtail), or did they go out of fashion before his time?

Although the books we turn to in our research are wonderfully illustrated, we will still find ourselves searching each picture for a uniform detail that seems to be just out of sight; a hand is blocking the view of a pocket, or the folds of a standard droop across its bearer's cross belt, hiding the buckle. Some problems constantly recur. When we take a photograph we rarely take a back view, and it's galling to find that most illustrators of books on military uniforms adopt the same approach. You will find front views, three-quarter front views, and the occasional back view; but when you are modelling a private soldier you will often be frustrated by being offered the back view of an officer, and then it's down to guesswork – presuming from the information you have got, for example, that the jacket tails and turnbacks are the same length and design for both ranks – or a dash to the library or bookshop.

I mention both, though in my experience few libraries have a large selection of suitable books on this subject, and I would recommend firstly a visit to a good second-hand bookshop, and then a look at the Osprey Men-at-Arms revolving display to be found in most good bookshops. Osprey are now part of Reed Books International, and most of their titles under the Men-at-Arms banner are constantly being reprinted. A collection of these outstanding quarto-sized paperback books will provide access to detailed information on uniforms worn by the Mongol and Byzantine armies, the Romans, the Samurai and many, many more, and there are Falklands War Specials describing the land, sea and air forces of that campaign.

For our purposes there are two titles of particular relevance. Number 107, *British Infantry Equipment 1808–1908*, has an excellent colour plate showing a corporal of the 2nd Battalion the 95th Rifles (1812) seated on a keg while loading his Baker rifle. Much of his equipment has been discarded. Over his green jacket he wears just a black waist belt (with the kind of snake buckle beloved of schoolboys), a crossover shoulder belt suspending a pouch on the right hip containing paper cartridges, ball and powder and, resting on that, a powder horn held by a cord strung through leather 'pipes' on the pouch belt. The sword bayonet is worn on the left side.

This figure is exactly right for our first toy soldier – a minimum of equipment, plenty of detail in the colour plate, and just four colours to consider: green for the jacket; black for the shako (hat), collar and cuffs, belts, boots and gaiters; grey for the trousers; and brown for the powder flask and rifle butt. When the time comes you will also need dabs of silver for the hat badge, and brass or gold for the bayonet hilt.

Men-at-Arms number 119, *Wellington's Infantry (2)*, is the

second title I recommend. This has some interesting information about the 95th Rifles and their precursors, an excellently detailed colour plate that shows our rifleman wearing full equipment and a lengthy descriptive text with much vital information.

Harking back to one of my questions, neither queues nor pigtails are mentioned in either book. In fact, powdering of the hair was abolished in the British army in 1795, 11-inch queues or pigtails were introduced the following year, and from 1808 hair was to be cut short.

3 The Toy Soldier: Modelling

With your materials and tools assembled on a firm work surface, the light moved into position, a good magnifying glass standing by and the anatomy chart and colour plates of the 95th Rifleman propped up before you, you are ready to commence modelling.

Quickly recapping, those of you who are modelling straight through from scratch will have before you a Minikin made from Plasticine, Fimo, or another material of your choice and, particularly in the case of Plasticine, you will from necessity continue in that material. Others who went on to Chapter 4 will have metal Minikins, and the nature of that material means that you must proceed using one of the epoxy putties – Milliput, Kneadatite or Sylmasta. There may be others on the market.

Throughout this section I will be concentrating on modelling with Milliput (although I realize other compounds will be in use, for simplicity I will use only that name), but when this excellent material is in its soft state it is very similar to Plasticine or any other soft modelling compound. In other words, most of my instructions can be followed by modellers using other compounds, and where there are important differences in technique, I will make it clear.

Procedures dealt with in this chapter are:

- step-by-step sculpting

- making equipment and accessories
- some thoughts on design

The Head

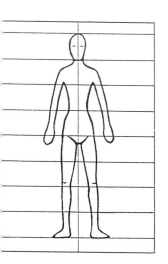

Personal choice has a lot to do with where you decide to start. I like to begin with the head for two reasons. First, by immediately creating a face, however small, with its own expression I am giving my tiny toy soldier a personality. Even within the 6.75 mm at your disposal it is possible to form recognizable scowls, smiles, or give the mouth a shape that, in conjunction with the set of the eyebrows, becomes a yell of anger or fear. Something as simple as the angle of the head helps further to establish the personality, and the whole effect – a revelation of the tiny figure's temperament – can be used as a guide when modelling the body: an arrogant face will lead to the erect body of a proud, haughty soldier, while a downcast expression will be reflected in a body that tends to slouch or slump.

The second reason is much more prosaic: by moulding the head first, I can conveniently hold the whole of the body in my hand!

The Minikin was the most basic of figures. On it you are now beginning the business of serious modelling, so always remember that you are working in three dimensions. Turn the small figure frequently, in your hands or on the turntable, viewing it from all angles. Before beginning the head, study people close to you (or a good piece of sculpture, if you have one). See the way the head sits on the neck when viewed from the front. Look at it from the side and do the same, comparing the bulge at the back of the skull with the forward thrust of the jaw. You will find that the line of the lower curve of the skull – at the nape of the neck – can be continued through to the front to form the jaw line. Note also the position of the ears in relation to the angle of the jaw.

Use your Milliput now to begin shaping the 95th Rifleman's head. This is ticklish work in which tiny balls of Milliput become enormous when pressed onto the Minikin's 6.75 mm head. Use your fingers to do the rough work, then one of your small modelling tools to form the important lower lines: back of skull, shape of jaw. If you find that freshly mixed Milliput sticks to the fingers or modelling tools, moisten them slightly with clean water. Leave the face smooth, and once you are satisfied with the overall shape – don't be too concerned about the top of the head; your soldier will be wearing a hat – you will need some measurements to guide you.

The eye sockets are set exactly midway between the chin and the top of the head. Press them in with a tool with a rounded point: a knitting needle is ideal. Bearing in mind the scale to which you are working, form the brows with the tiniest piece of Milliput, rolled thin. Press it on, and use a small tool to smooth the upper edge of the brows into the forehead. Their lower edge will form a slight projection.

A nice easy way of establishing the length of the nose is to take another tiny roll of Milliput, press it into position between the brows, and cut it off exactly halfway between brows and chin. Again, use your modelling tool to form a pleasing shape.

Two tiny balls of Milliput can be pressed onto the face on either side of the nose, and blended in to form cheekbones.

The mouth comes halfway between nose and chin. Take a tiny piece of Milliput and form it into a slight mound in that position – very slight! – then blend it into the cheeks and chin. With a sharp modelling tool, form the lips. This is one area that gives me some difficulty, usually because I have made the nose too long and left myself insufficient room to form the mouth and chin. So remember that measurement: the length of the nose is equal to half the distance between *brows* and chin, not between eyes and chin.

Ears are virtually impossible to model in detail, but this is in any case unnecessary on a 54 mm toy soldier. The key thing is to be meticulous about their position, use balls of Milliput flattened onto the sides of the skull, form a rough ear shape and leave it at that. You can, if you wish, lift the top and back edges slightly. Their length is roughly equivalent to the nose.

The hat worn by the NCOs and men of the 95th Rifles in 1812 was a slightly tapered shako with a rounded or very slightly squared peak. (The officer's version had a much squarer peak, which could be folded back.) Once in position on your toy soldier the shako's lower edge – and thus the peak – will be just above the eyebrows, so you will need a cylinder of Milliput with a hollow in its base so that it sits over the head's crown. In height the shako is slightly taller than the distance from its lower rim to the soldier's chin. You must judge the peak by reference to the colour plates and by using your eyes to establish a pleasing balance: you want a reasonable projection, but not a baseball cap!

Discussing the peak of the soldier's shako leads inevitably to the different modelling techniques that can be adopted with Milliput and the permanently soft materials like Plasticine. With Plasticine you are forced to do all your fine finishing with hard modelling tools, and care must always be taken to avoid touching completed sections – especially projections like the shako's peak. Milliput has an enormous advantage. It is slightly more difficult to work with initially, but fine finishing such as that needed around the eyebrows, nose and lips can be done with a fine artists' paintbrush moistened with water. With such a delicate tool quite amazing results can be achieved on the tiniest of parts, and because Milliput sets iron-hard in about four hours, they are permanent. Plasticine can also to a certain extent be worked with a paintbrush. But instead of moistening the brush with water, white spirit must be used – and without due care the modelling material degenerates into a horrible slime.

Deciding how the shako's peak should be finished provides a good example of Milliput's versatility. It's perfectly possible to work as one would with Plasticine by shaping the peak with a modelling tool, then finishing off Milliput-style with a moistened paint brush. But an alternative method is to shape the peak only roughly, wait for the Milliput to harden, then finish the peak by carving and scraping into shape with a sharp craft knife or grinding with a suitable cutter in a Mini-drill.

The 95th Rifle's cockade – a small green tuft – sticks up from the top of the hat (front/centre) and is best added when all other modelling is complete.

At this point we are back with our previous question of how much detail to include. You have created a recognizable face, and placed a hat upon the head. How are you going to represent the hair which is visible at the back of the head, and around the ears?

It is just possible to model it, albeit in a crude way. Work with minute pieces of Milliput, create the hair as a smooth, slightly raised area shaped at the nape of the neck and around the ears, then score its surface all over with a sharp knife. I would recommend doing that, but the alternative is to ignore the hair entirely and add it at the painting stage. For a toy soldier this is a perfectly viable option.

One further tip before we move on. A lot of modelling work on toy soldiers involves minute balls and sausages of Milliput. Instead of fiddling about with blunt fingers, use the sharp point of a modelling knife to transfer them from your work surface to their final position.

The Body   A good rule to follow when modelling or painting is to *work from the skin outwards*. As far as modelling goes, all this means is that you start with a naked figure, and clothe it. In the case of the 95th Rifleman, you will dress your Minikin in his jacket, trousers and boots, give him his belt, pouch belt and powder horn and, finally, place a Baker rifle in his right hand.

Your Minikin was made in a sort of adaptable, gingerbread man non-position – legs slightly apart, arms a little away from the body. My suggested pose for your first figure is 'at attention', so before beginning modelling work on the body, bring the legs together and press the arms close to the sides. Now think about your soldier's attitude and personality, issues whose implications we discussed when modelling the head. When I was in the army we were told to march with a swagger – chin up, chest out, arms swinging hard back as well as forwards. Although your figure won't be in a marching position, it's still possible to give it a military bearing by slightly arching the back and squaring the shoulders (that will need to be done in the early modelling, rather than by trying to make adjustments at a later stage when fine detail has been added and the body is in any case immovable).

Once again the modelling is a process of adding small lumps and thin slices of Milliput to the figure so that it begins to take shape as a uniformed member of the 95th Rifles. This time when you begin you will experience a feeling of relief, for instead of working with bits of modelling material not much bigger than a pin head you will be able to use comparatively large amounts. But not for your first task. Adopting the principle of working from the skin outwards, first use your Milliput to form the shape of the stock at your soldier's neck. This is a band of material worn around the neck, but all you need do is make a shape that looks like the front bit of a polo-neck or roll-collar sweater, tucked up under the chin. The back and sides will be covered by the jacket's collar.

Now it's on with the bulkier work. Some modellers complete one section – let's say the jacket – and move on to the next. With the head completed I think it's advisable to work on the rest of the figure as a whole, constantly turning

The Minikin has now been taken a stage further. The toy soldier's face has been modelled, and some uniform details have been added. Still no hands or feet!

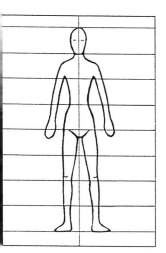

it so that proportions are maintained and a suitably arrogant or haughty pose is achieved.

You will be guided by your colour plates and by the measurements on your anatomy chart. Remember shoulder widths, the slightly narrower hips (and their important halfway position), the position of the waist (navel) and knees. Jackets are usually depicted as being of a good fit (in my opinion there is always some artistic licence), so try to visualize the shape of the body beneath the clothing: the bulge of the chest, the slight concavity below the ribs, the way shoulder blades are two separate shapes (not overdone) and how, at attention, the back will be slightly arched. Trousers, too, are best thought of as tight fitting, although often these were baggier grey overalls. In the case of trousers the buttocks will be quite clearly defined, as will the heavy thigh muscles and the bulge of the calves.

Sharp lines to look for come at the edges of the collar, the lower edge of the jacket, the cuffs, and the bottom edge of the trousers. Note that the front of the jacket is cut at waist level, curving gently down towards and around the hips to form a short squared flap that falls over the buttocks. This could easily involve us in the intricacies of jacket turnbacks and so forth, but they are not too important as we are working on a simplified toy soldier and in any case equipment such as a pouch and bayonet will hide some of those details.

At the clearly defined edges mentioned, Plasticine will be cut with a sharp craft knife which will at once create a neat finish. You will have discovered by now that soft Milliput does not readily form a sharp edge and, where one is needed – at the collar, cuffs, and the lower edge of the trousers – I would recommend leaving the finishing until the material is quite firm and can be neatly sliced. The lower edge of the jacket, however, will need a softer outline, so in this case the Milliput should be cut earlier, then worked on with the moistened paint brush.

Other sharp edges will be noticed on the sleeves above the cuffs – where the contrasting black colour tapers to a vee pointing up the outside of the forearm – and at the shoulder epaulettes. But these are more examples of optional refinements and, like the modelling of head hair, can safely be left to the painting stage.

Finally, there is the line down the front of the jacket where the two sides overlap. This can be defined at Milliput's soft stage by running a flat modelling tool down the chest in a straight line, pressing gently so that one side of the jacket is left standing slightly proud of the other. If you decide to do this, remember that men's jackets fasten left over right.

Buttons can be represented as tiny blobs of silver paint at the finishing stage, although a hollow punch of the right size, or the tip of a retracted ball pen or propelling pencil, pressed against soft Milliput works very well.

Because the legs are together and the arms pressed close to the sides, there are no wide open spaces to cause concern. But you are trying to give a faithful representation of a soft material, so even with a simple toy soldier it's well worth studying the way a uniform or suit hangs on the human body, and the creases and folds that are formed in different positions. If you are a man you need simply pose, suitably attired, before a mirror; if a woman, ask brother, boyfriend or husband to act as a male model. Nothing looks worse than creases wrongly depicted, so be cautious, and minimize rather than exaggerate. Your toy soldier is standing to attention so there will be no wrinkles at the inside of the elbow. There will be one or two where the trousers pull at the leg fork, and if you have allowed the trousers to rest on the boots, there will be some there. Remember, however, that these are optional refinements; a toy soldier often sneers at such attention to detail, and stands haughty and wrinkle-free!

The feet should be modelled pointing slightly outwards (but see 'The Base', p.38). Like all of Wellington's infantry the 95th Rifles wore boots covered by gaiters. Because both are black, there is no way of differentiating between these at the painting stage, so it is best to ignore the gaiters altogether.

The left hand should be formed into a fist, the back of the hand outwards, thumb to the front. The right hand should also have the back of the hand outwards, but the fingers should be straight and, if possible, there should be a gap between fingers and thumb so that the Baker rifle can be held.

Equipment

The equipment worn by our 95th Rifleman consists of one cross or pouch belt, a sword bayonet suspended from a waist belt, an ammunition pouch and a powder horn (or flask).

Both belts can be formed from a strip of Milliput that has been allowed to become firm, rolled like pastry on a powdered surface, then cut to the required width. If you like you can roll a wide sheet of Milliput and from that cut the belts to the exact width. Drape the cross belt over the left shoulder and bring the ends across the chest and back to meet just behind the right hip. At the rear the belt will come neatly across the back from the shoulder to the correct point behind the hip. At the front the right arm is in the way when the belt comes down across the chest, so here cut it at an angle so that it appears to pass under the arm. Press the belt smoothly to the surface of the uniform on the chest and back.

The waist belt goes on next, wrapped around the soldier to meet at the centre front. Again, you will need to cut it so that it appears to pass under the arms. At the front, allow a fraction of the lower edge of the jacket to show beneath the belt.

Sometimes it is difficult to get belts to sit neatly when formed from firm Milliput in this way, so an alternative method is to use soft Milliput – it sticks in place much better – and create the shape of the belts by cutting their long edges with a sharp craft knife. Once the Milliput has fully hardened, the surface of the belts can be made flat and smooth by scraping with a craft knife followed by a final rubbing with fine wet-and-dry paper.

I mentioned earlier that the powder flask was suspended from a cord threaded through leather pipes on the cross or pouch belt, and rested on the cartridge pouch. For ease of modelling I suggest the cartridge pouch and powder flask are made as one piece. The pouch will be a small oblong of Milliput, with flap details as simple or as refined as you care to make them. The powder flask can be made from a small, tapered roll of Milliput, curved to the required shape and attached to the outside face of the pouch.

A quick word here about the way one piece of equipment can be joined to another – or, indeed, a nose fixed to a face, a pack or haversack attached to a soldier's back. Let's use the latter as an example. The oblong pack is placed on the flat of the soldier's back, so that the side and lower edges on the inner surface of the pack are against the soldier's back (the upper edge is likely to be a little above the figure's shoulders). Now, with a modelling tool, fix the pack firmly to the soldier's back by squashing or nipping a tiny bit of Milliput all the way along the length of each edge and squashing it against the soldier's back, forming a neat, joinless 'seam'.

Use this method to fix the powder flask to the cartridge pouch, then do the same again to fix the cartridge pouch to the soldier, positioning it behind the right hip so that it appears to be suspended from the pouch belt. You would think that, unlike in the pack example used above, the shape of pouch and hip means that the pouch cannot lie completely flat. In fact the cartridge pouch is much smaller than a back pack, your soldier's hip and right buttock will be quite bulky, the right side of the pouch will be against the soldier's clamped right arm and you will be able to use the 'seaming' method to great effect.

The powder flask's carrying cord – if it is represented at all – is best added at the painting stage as a fine brown line down the centre of the pouch belt.

The Base

All toy soldiers stand on their own integral base. This can be square, round, oval – even irregular – and should be designed to balance harmoniously with the figure's overall size. Being integral it should be made from the same material as the soldier. A good thickness is about 2 mm.

Working with Milliput, you will need to fashion an oblong of that thickness, slightly over-size, and use the seaming method to fix your soldier to his base. To do this effectively it is best to blend the feet into the base rather than the reverse, so it's a good idea to work on the feet and the base at the same time. Milliput's slow curing properties make this quite feasible, and the advantage of adopting this method is that you can begin with over-size feet and squash the excess material on to the base as you establish their correct size and shape.

With the soldier attached to his base you can now use a craft knife to cut it to its correct size. Once the Milliput has hardened, final finishing can be done with a file to give the base a neat, square edge.

If you have worked with Plasticine throughout you will need to adopt a slightly different procedure. The two leg portions of the armature wire will still be projecting through the underside of the heels, and you can now clip these off so that just 2 mm remains to press down into the Plasticine base. The seaming works exactly the same as with Milliput.

Incidentally, those readers who are not going to attempt mould-making, and are worried about their collection of Plasticine soldiers being permanently malleable might be interested in remarks on this subject by

The Plasticine figure nears completion. A base and feet have been added, and the trousers roughly shaped. The arms have been cut to approximately the correct length (the armature wire can be seen protruding from their ends)

Arthur Taylor in his excellent paperback book *Discovering Model Soldiers*. Mr Taylor mentions Mr W.A. Thorburn, then Keeper of the Scottish United Services Museum, who made many models from Plasticine, applied a coat of varnish before painting them in enamels and matt paints, and who was able to report that several were as good as new some twenty years after they were made. This little story might also offer some relief to readers who were wondering if Plasticine could be painted.

Weapons Our 95th Rifleman is armed with a Baker rifle and a sword bayonet. Modellers working in Plasticine or Milliput who have no intention of mould-making will attach these to their toy soldiers at once; those working on a figure that is to be a master from which a silicone rubber mould will be made will make the weapons and put them to one side. Indeed, these too will be masters, for many more weapons will be needed as a collection grows.

Making weapons is a challenge to ingenuity, yet that challenge can be tempered if the theme running through this book is kept firmly in mind: simplicity. Remember it, especially at times like this, when you are faced with the task of modelling a rifle whose flintlock is equivalent in size to your soldier's little finger. I have seen toy soldiers with rifles or muskets that look like pick helves with a trigger guard tacked on, others that are masterpieces of miniature modelling. Somewhere between these extremes lies a happy medium, and to achieve it you will use bits of iron wire, ice-lolly sticks – anything and everything that looks as if, with a little of that ingenuity, it can be turned into a weapon.

Details of the Baker rifle are best taken from the second of the recommended books, *Wellington's Infantry (2)*. An excellent black-and- white plate shows the rifle and its bayonet, one above the other. With our 95th Rifleman at attention the butt of his Baker rifle will be against the outside of his right foot, while the muzzle will be aligned with a point a little way above his right elbow. You will see from the plate that the barrel is a little more than twice the length of the wooden stock. If you are carving it from an ice-lolly stick, leave a solid trigger guard, and because your soldier is at attention it's as well to depict the sling as being pulled tight – simply represent it as a flat strip lying under the barrel, from trigger guard to just before the muzzle.

By the by, an excellent material that I have only just discovered is the fine lead wire sold in good fishing shops. It comes in several thicknesses, and is apparently used by fly fishermen to add some weight to their lures. It can be used for a variety of purposes when modelling toy soldiers: simply by drawing the solid handle of a craft knife along the soft metal flattens it, and thin belts – or the rifle sling just mentioned – can be formed in this way.

There is a fine picture of the Baker rifle's sword bayonet in *British Infantry Equipment 1808–1908*, while some idea of its size can be obtained from study of the illustrations in *Wellington's Infantry (2)*. These should be sufficient. There are books giving precise details of all weapons used throughout the British army's long history, but for our purposes it's enough to know that when suspended from the waist belt, the tip of the sword bayonet's scabbard will hang a little above the back of your soldier's left knee.

One way of making the bayonet is to take a piece of soft wire and hammer it into a strip, leaving a tiny round section at one end for the hilt. Again, the lead wire just mentioned can be used, although for a bayonet it is probably a little soft. The other end should be filed to a point. The wire knucklebow would be almost impossible to cast at this scale, though if you are making your bayonet by hand to attach to your soldier some delicate work with fine fuse wire can produce an excellent result. Otherwise, my suggestion is to dispense with the knucklebow; indeed, the text in the recommended book mentions contemporary pictures that show bayonets so modified by serving soldiers.

The above methods can be used to produce finished weapons, or masters for later reproduction. Don't worry too much if the delicacy of the work is at present beyond you. Paint works wonders, and both rifle and bayonet – however crude – are transformed when the overall black or brown colour is highlighted with brilliant touches of brass paint.

Some Thoughts on Design

Within the constraints of the (deceptive) simplicity that many consider to be the hallmark and charm of the toy soldier, there is ample scope for individual modellers to bring freshness and originality to their creations.

John Ruddle's *Collectors' Guide to Britains Model Soldiers* is an interesting book that clearly demonstrates the charm of even the simplest figures. Britains began production in the 1800s with hollow-cast models made from tin alloy, and switched to plastic in the 1960s. From the colour and monochrome plates in Mr Ruddle's book it is obvious that many of their early toy soldiers were extremely crudely modelled with almost slapdash painting (though sets with higher-quality painting were available to order). But in those days they *were* toys, and even though arms seemed to bend like rubber, legs took impossible strides and Soudanese (sic) Infantry were given enormous white eyes with a black dot in the centre, these soldiers were dashing and romantic; detachments of Skinner's Horse or the 1st Bengal Cavalry must have brought a gleam to many a boy's eye when set up and stretched out at full gallop across a living-room carpet!

My own 'Union Jacks' first appeared in the early 1980s, and I like to believe that the 1751 grenadier companies with which I started were among the first toy soldiers – designed though they were for collectors – that approached connoisseur figures in the quality of their castings and painting. The castings were acknowledged by a respected American writer to be superior to Britains, and the paintwork on the mitre caps included fine detailing that can be seen to advantage only through a magnifying glass.

A logical question arises from this. If toy soldiers are always meant to be viewed *en masse*, why bother with painstaking detail?

It's a valid point, and I offer two answers. Firstly, the *en masse* theory applies only to collectors who are building up large thematic displays; other collectors will keep each set of soldiers on a glass shelf in an illuminated display cabinet, or even in its original box. Secondly, and perhaps most importantly, there is the modellers' pride in their work, and the determination to produce only the best.

Between the two extremes – the simple toy soldier whose sophistication is on a par with those early Britains; the toy soldier trying hard to be a connoisseur figure – there are endless possibilities for the imaginative modeller.

You will to a great extent be guided by your own reasons for producing toy soldiers. For example, if you intend to reproduce the Trooping the Colour, your soldiers will necessarily be dressed in parade ground splendour, stand rigidly to attention or march with that swagger I have already mentioned.

However, if the 95th Rifleman has fired your imagination and you would like to produce dioramas (small three-dimensional scenes) representing incidents in Peninsular War battles such as Vimiera or Talavera, then you can give free rein to your imagination with these and the other regiments involved. A photograph in Arthur Taylor's little book actually shows a group of riflemen of the 95th Foot – by Charles Stadden – and in both the modelling and painting he has created battle-weary individuals with haunted faces who wear bloodstained bandages, patched uniforms, and are obviously a long way away from any parade ground.

So once again I have given you two extremes, and from these and my previous suggestions you will see that toy soldiers can be all things to all people. The choices available to you as you sit down at your work bench lie somewhere between parade ground spit-and-polish and dishevelled soldiers caked in the mud and blood of war; and, always, you can approach your modelling comforted by the thought that, in the world of toy soldiers, simple figures are often the best.

4 Mass Production: Masters and Moulds

So far throughout this book I have been differentiating between those modellers who are content to make all their toy soldiers in one process, beginning with the wire armature and ending with the finished figure, and others who want to build up a collection much more quickly and so jump ahead to mould-making. I have used this approach because, as always, it's a case of horses for courses. However, I do firmly believe that while many modellers may dispense with the Minikin – preferring instead to make each master figure from scratch – the vast majority will turn to mould-making sooner rather than later. It is a wonderful way of producing whole armies of figures that are exact replicas of each other and it is a craft in itself. To those critics who might point out, with some justification, that it is not modelling in the true sense of the word I can only reply, yes, but what a joy it is to see those glittering castings emerge.

When compiling a book such as this it's inevitable that there will be occasions when one must backtrack. That happens here, because not only must the mould be suitable for the master figure, the reverse is also true. Figures in certain poses can only be reproduced from a mould with great difficulty, so I'm going to occupy a little space at the beginning of the chapter in further discussion of the design of master figures.

We begin with that, but will also cover much more:

- more on master figure design
- malleable master figures
- silicone rubber for moulds
- re-usable mould boxes
- pouring a one-piece mould
- cutting to extract the master figure
- making a two-piece mould
- complicated moulds

Our rifleman of the 95th Foot was posed deliberately at attention to avoid the problems that can be faced when making moulds for figures in more imaginative poses. The reasons why such a figure is easy to reproduce may not be obvious, so let's look at mould-making in a little more detail.

More on Master Figure Design

Your aim is to build up a collection of figures, many of which will be identical. To do that quickly and easily you need a master figure that can be used to make a mould, then removed from that mould leaving both figure and mould undamaged.

One method, called the lost wax (*cire perdue*) process, has no such refinements. Using this technique, a figure (or other object) is sculpted from wax, and in the sculpting a projection is left – let's say it is a thin rod extending vertically from the top of the head. The figure is then completely immersed in a mould-making compound, through which the projection is allowed to protrude. When the mould is hard, heat is applied to the outside so that the wax figure melts: the boiling wax is then expelled from the opening once occupied by the projection. Molten metal is now poured in and allowed to solidify. The mould is then shattered, leaving a perfectly formed metal figure.

This is still an excellent process for the production of figures that are going to be of some value: an artistic bronze, for example. Obviously, toy soldiers can be made in this way too. The problem is that all you gain is a tin-alloy figure to replace the one made of wax – and the whole process of sculpting and mould-making must begin again.

Your master figures will be made of Milliput. They are hard, almost unbreakable, and *they will have undercut sections* – the backward slope beneath a prominent chin, for example, or that beneath a soldier's peaked cap when his head is lowered. This is quite all right, because the mould-making material you will be working with is flexible silicone rubber, which can be pulled away from all but the most severe undercuts. Nevertheless, a silicone rubber mould can be damaged, because it is bound to be more delicate than an inflexible master figure – and you want to use it again and again.

When designing your master figure, you need to balance the imaginative posing of your toy soldier against the practical problems of extracting it from a mould. A figure standing erect with arms akimbo creates only minor problems: the two closed holes between arms and body that will be filled by the silicone rubber are in the same plane. A figure sitting on a cask, bent forward, with his left arm on his hip, his right elbow on right knee and his head supported by that hand, would create devilish problems: the holes between the left arm and body, and between the right arm and head/right arm and leg, are now on different planes (and there is still the hole between legs and cask to consider!).

Makers of the larger connoisseur figures get around this problem by making their military figures in bits and pieces. Torsos, legs and arms are often cast separately, and the military modeller buys the figure in kit form and gets much enjoyment from its assembly. Toy soldier manufacturers often cast the right arm separately (keeping faith with tradition), and attach it to a rather ugly projection on the right shoulder.

With the figure we are producing we will experience no problems. There are no spaces between arms and body, or between the legs. There should be few undercuts. We could have further simplified the soldier by modelling the sword bayonet flat against the left leg, but I have suggested casting both weapons separately because it will give you practice in mould-making and provide the beginnings of a small armoury.

Malleable Master Figures While master figures made of Milliput or some other hard compound are ideal because of their durability, those made from Plasticine also present no insurmountable problems. Indeed, I used Plasticine originals for the first three or four sets of figures in my Union Jacks range. If there is one glaring fault it is that the Plasticine tends to stick to the silicone rubber, so that before casting, the inside of the mould must be scraped clean, then washed with a paintbrush dipped in white spirits.

With all malleable master figures it is essential to have simple poses because, as you will discover later, they are too delicate to withstand the rigours of two-piece mould-making. In any case they will almost certainly be damaged in some way during any kind of mould-making, so with this type of master figure you must get the mould right first time.

The first figure you cast from that mould will become the master figure from which all future moulds will be made. You can now put your Plasticine original – battered, scarred, but still a record of your modelling skills – in a place of honour on your workroom shelf.

Silicone Rubber for Moulds

General Electric's cold-cure, room temperature vulcanizing silicone rubbers such as RTV-11 and RTV-31, are the model-maker's dream come true. They can be bought in handy 1 lb packs which contain silicone rubber and a suitable catalyst. The silicone rubber is initially a free-flowing solution, but when the catalyst is added it begins to 'cure' and after a period of time becomes a strong, flexible rubber similar to that found in a good quality eraser. Catalysts available include DBT, which gives a cure time of between 24 and 48 hours, and Beta 1 and Beta 2, which can reduce the cure time to under one hour. In the simplest mould-making procedure – perfectly satisfactory for our 95th Rifleman – the rubber and catalyst are mixed together, and the catalysed rubber poured into a suitable leak-proof box in the centre of which our soldier is standing to attention. The soldier is completely immersed. When the catalysed rubber has cured, the flexible rubber mould can be removed from the box and the toy soldier cut free using a sharp craft knife.

Re-Usable Mould Boxes

A 54 mm toy soldier, plus base and hat, can stand an impressive 65 mm tall, overall. To make a mould that will be effective and long-lasting your soldier must be totally immersed in silicone rubber, with at least 15 mm of rubber above the top of his hat – preferably more. So your mould box should be 90 mm high. You must also allow ample space all around the soldier. This seems to imply that in area the box can be quite small; after all, our rifleman is rigidly at attention, and will take up little room. However, you want to build a box that will take figures in many different poses, and as a toy soldier's integral base can be up to 40 mm wide and a soldier posed with his rifle or musket at the aim can measure, horizontally, 60 mm from the back edge of the base to the rifle muzzle, I suggest your box should be 100 mm square (exterior measurements).

The simplest mould box will therefore consist of five loose panels, four of them 90 mm x 100 mm, the fifth somewhat bigger – about 130 mm square. Cut this and two of the 90 mm x 100 mm panels from plywood – three-ply is ideal – and two from something a little thicker (about 10 mm), with their edges neatly squared; for the box shown in the illustration (p.47) I used chipboard. The flat surfaces and edges of all the panels should be smoothed with sandpaper. An open-topped box is formed by

The completed master figure standing alongside a simple mould box made from plywood and chipboard

standing the two thick panels (on their long edges) on your work surface to form the ends, and placing the two thinner plywood panels – again on their longer edges – against them to form the sides. If the end panels are about 10 mm thick, the interior measurement will be reduced by that amount at either end (because the two ends stand inside the sides), giving an interior measurement of 100 mm x 80 mm. This slightly rectangular shape is ideal, because a soldier will always measure more one way than the other (even if only because of an oblong base).

Once formed, the box can be secured by strong elastic bands, or by binding with twine or thin wire. Because the two ends are thick and have square edges, it will retain its shape. It will certainly be strong enough to hold the curing silicone rubber. The 130 mm-square panel forms the base, and for the moment remains unattached.

Positioning and securing the four loose panels can be fiddly, so a more sophisticated version of this box will save time when you have a lot of soldiers to cast. The improved box is made from exactly the same materials – two 90 mm x 100 mm panels forming the sides, two thicker panels of the same size forming the ends and a larger one for the base. Again, use sandpaper to smooth all surfaces and edges. This time, however, take one of the side panels and, using a fretsaw or coping saw, cut two horizontal slots inwards from one 90 mm edge. The first should be 30 mm from the top, the second 30 mm from the bottom. Each should be about 5 mm wide and 20 mm long. Do the same with the other side panel. You will be left with two side panels looking like very chunky capital Es.

Now permanently secure the first thick end panel *inside* the two prepared side panels – at their non-slotted edges – using a good adhesive and panel pins. You will have formed a strong three-sided box, with horizontal slots in the two side panels – equidistant from top and bottom – at the open end.

Take the remaining end panel, and hold it with one 90 mm edge towards you. Drill two horizontal holes squarely into this first 90 mm edge, rotate the panel horizontally through 180 degrees and drill two identical holes into the second 90 mm edge. Each hole, like the slots in the sides, should be located 30 mm from the bottom and 30 mm from the top. Check that when you slide this end panel into position to complete your box, you can see the two holes in each edge through the respective slots in the side panels.

Take the end panel out again, obtain four bolts and, with a hacksaw, cut off the heads. Coat half the length of each of the modified bolts with a strong adhesive such as Araldite and insert them into the four holes to form projecting, threaded studs. Make sure they are sufficiently long so that when the end panel is again slid into position, each of the four studs protrudes through one of the slots in the side panels. Finally, once the adhesive has dried, this loose end panel can be slid into position and secured by fitting a washer and wing-nut to each of the studs.

To make a simple one-piece mould for your rifleman of the 95th Foot you will need:

Pouring a One-piece Mould

- the master figure
- one simple or improved mould box
- silicone rubber, with catalyst
- a mixing container and stirrer
- rubber gloves
- Plasticine

Note that master figure also means Minikin, because this is the method you would use to produce a host of those simple figures.

The rubber gloves are optional. All silicone rubbers come with handling instructions, warnings about toxic properties and procedures to be followed to ensure the materials are handled with complete safety.

Preparation   Your box should be assembled either by binding the four loose sides of the simple box with twine or thin wire or by sliding the loose end panel of the improved box into position and tightening the wing-nuts. The base of the box can be fixed into position with Plasticine. Place one open end of your assembled box centrally on the base panel, roll a long, thin sausage of Plasticine and fix the base into position by applying the Plasticine all around the outside of the join between base and box as if you were plugging the gap between a wash basin and tiled wall. Apply the Plasticine firmly, ensuring that there are no gaps through which the liquid silicone rubber can flow.

This method has its problems, as RTV-11 is particularly liquid and will seep through the tiniest cracks. You may have better ideas. If your mould box is particularly well made it may be possible to place strips of double-sided adhesive tape on the base, and press the mould box firmly in position. I have tried this method, and it does work well.

The side and end panels of your box should fit quite snugly, obviating the need to seal all edges with Plasticine. However, one good trick that proves effective with the simple box is to assemble it with packing tape – the wide, brown plastic type that normally comes in a large roll. Four long pieces can be used as effective seals on the outside four corners, while a fifth piece wrapped tightly around the assembled box will make everything secure.

There is no need to apply any kind of freeing compound or release agent to the inside surfaces of the box. The silicone rubber will stick slightly as it cures, but if you have smoothed the wooden surfaces it will pull away easily. If you want to use a release agent to be on the safe side, I can recommend Ambersil DP100.

The silicone rubber should be mixed according to the instructions supplied, usually so many drops of catalyst per 100 gms of rubber, the proportion to be varied according to the cure time required – between 24 and 48 hours. If you are using RTV-11 you will find the rubber is white, the DBT catalyst colourless. With RTV-31 the colours will be red and colourless respectively. Pour the rubber into your mixing container, add the catalyst and stir well. The aim is for a smooth, creamy consistency of a uniform colour. Mixing is somewhat hit and miss when using the colourless DBT catalyst, much easier with Beta 1 and Beta 2 which have distinctive colours. But whichever catalyst you use, do make sure that you stir right to the bottom of the mixing container.

The main problem you will encounter when making moulds with silicone rubber is that the mixed solution contains hundreds of tiny air bubbles that, at the later casting stage, will leave your gleaming toy soldier pimpled with tiny, unwanted balls of metal.   *Air Bubbles*

Air bubbles cannot be avoided altogether, but the problem is exacerbated by over-enthusiastic mixing. You should mix thoroughly but gently, being careful not to lift folds of silicone rubber that will trap pockets of air. (There are vacuum devices that remove air bubbles from mixed solutions, but they are quite expensive.)

The master figure – either the virgin malleable figure or the silicone-rubber-coated rigid figure – should now be placed within the centre of the box. You have given your mould box an oblong base, its length in line with your figure's shoulders, so stand him in the centre of the box facing one of the longer end panels (the removable one if you are using the improved box), so that there will be the maximum thickness of rubber on all sides. Placing the figure so that you know exactly where he is will also make it easy to cut him out of the finished mould.   *Pouring*

If necessary, make a pencil mark on the inside of the box indicating the final level of the silicone rubber. If you have a figure sporting a tall hat, this mark will be very close to the top of the box.

It might be advisable to secure the figure in some way – perhaps with a minute dab of a suitable adhesive beneath the base – though I have never found it necessary. The thinking behind this is that when thick silicone rubber (it tends to be thick at lower temperatures) is poured around a light toy soldier, the figure can be pushed to one side. My own feeling is that you can get around this by pressing one finger on the top of your soldier's head while you pour gently with the other hand. Once the rubber solution has begun to rise, its weight will hold the figure in position.

Air bubbles can also form during the pouring stage, when the thickish rubber rises quickly inside the mould box and is unable to fill the tiny spaces and fissures that will be found all over your

Pouring the catalysed silicone rubber into the corner of the mould box. The master figure stands in the centre. This box has been sealed with parcel tape and Plasticine

toy soldier: under the chin, beneath a cap's peak, between the legs, in the tiny V at the centre of a stiff collar. You can minimize the problem by pouring the silicone rubber slowly into the corner of the mould box and letting it flow around the master figure and gradually rise up the legs and body. Stop several times to allow any trapped air to rise to the surface.

With a malleable master figure, there is not much else you can do. If you are working with a rigid master figure you can eliminate the air bubble problem almost entirely if, prior to pouring, you use a medium stiff brush to work some of the silicone rubber solution into nooks and crannies in your soldier where bubbles are likely to form.

Just to repeat the basic procedure. Pour slowly but steadily into one corner of the mould box, allowing the rubber solution to flow across the box's base and around the soldier. As the solution rises up the figure stop pouring occasionally in order to allow trapped bubbles of air to escape. Indeed, if you watch very closely you will see the rubber solution approaching problem areas such as the fork of the legs or recesses between arms and body, and you should slow or stop pouring then to allow those tiny areas to be filled.

Once the silicone rubber has been poured to your satisfaction, put the filled mould box where it won't be knocked (be careful if you do move it!) and get on with another task while the rubber cures.

Cutting to Extract the Master Figure

Curing times vary and can be affected by temperature. If you are impatient, putting the mould box in a warm room will help. I have sometimes greatly hastened the curing by using a fan heater. But whether you wait patiently or accelerate the process in some way, once the rubber has cured you can remove it from the mould box and start cutting to remove the master figure.

Scrape away the Plasticine and pull off the base of the box, then remove the twine, wire or parcel tape and pull away each side in turn. Do this gently; it's rather like pulling adhesive plaster off skin, and makes a similar ripping noise! With the improved box you will unscrew the wing-nuts and slide that end away, then prise the block of rubber out of the open-ended box.

Knowing where the master figure is located is important. Your 95th Rifleman is standing to attention, and you want to cut the mould into two neat halves so that the line of the cut goes down the sides of the soldier's shako, down through his ears, along the centre line of each shoulder and down his arms, then straight down the sides of his legs where you would expect to find a trouser seam. In other words, you want to finish up with two halves of a mould, each with concavities of the same depth, which represent, respectively, the front and rear halves of your soldier.

You can see where the soldier's base is, because if you turn the solid block of cured silicone rubber upside down there it is, flush with the bottom (silicone rubber may have seeped between it and the base of the box to form a thin skin; this should be pulled off). But starting your cut at the base is not a good idea; its large flat area tends to hide the rest of the soldier, and when cutting

The simple mould box, with the master figure completely immersed in the silicone rubber solution

blind you can easily stray off line.

When compared with the base, the head is a much smaller projection. It hides none of the soldier, and is a good point to aim for. If you positioned the soldier in the centre of the mould box, you know that his head will be about one inch down from an imaginary centre line drawn across the long width of the top of the mould block. With that knowledge to guide you, take a sharp craft knife and make a shallow cut in the block right along that imaginary centre line, from one edge of the block to the other. Your cut will be in line with the shoulders. Gradually deepen that cut, using your fingers to hold the gash open. As soon as your knife blade touches the top of the master figure's head (or shako), you know where you are and can cut with greater confidence.

With the head located you continue to cut, following the

imaginary line down one side of the soldier as detailed above – ears, shoulders, arms and so on. I find it helpful if I make a shallow cut all the way round one side of the block (let's say it's the left side), from the now clearly defined cut across the top, down the side – in line with the position you now know the soldier to be in – and along the bottom to the centre of one edge of the base.

Cut down the left side of the head (taking great care if the master figure is malleable), still using your fingers to hold the cut open and continuing the cut to the outside of the block. Cut along the top of the left shoulder and again cut to the block's edge. All is now plain sailing. As more of the soldier is revealed the cut becomes easier to hold open, and the sharp blade of your knife will slip easily down the arm, down the back of the hand, on to the trouser seam and so down the outside of the leg to the boots and base.

Once the left side of your soldier has been revealed, you have a choice. You can pull the soldier out of the mould through the slit you have made on the left of the mould block (this is easier to do when you are working with a rigid master figure), and divide the mould into two halves by cutting through the right side from the inside. Or you can leave the soldier exactly where he is and cut down the right side from the outside, following the line of the gradually exposed soldier just as you did before.

I would advise the latter course. You are less likely to damage the silicone rubber mould if you gently separate two halves than if you try dragging the soldier through a slit in his silicone rubber womb.

The negative images of your soldier on the inside of the mould should now be cleaned of Plasticine, first by careful picking and scraping, and finally by washing with a paintbrush soaked in white spirit. The mould should then be dried, and put to one side until you are ready to begin casting.

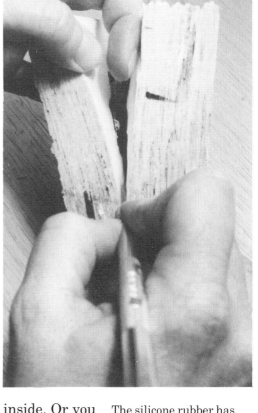

The silicone rubber has cured, and the mould removed from the mould box. Here, the master figure is being extracted by cutting through the mould with a craft knife. Note the way the fingers are used to widen the opening so that the cut can accurately follow the embedded master figure

Making a Two-piece Mould

One-piece moulds are quick and easy to make, and when used to reproduce a simple figure like our 95th Rifleman they will provide perfectly acceptable replicas. But one-piece moulds have two weaknesses. Firstly, if you have designed a figure standing in anything other than a simple pose, it can be devilishly tricky to cut free; imagine cutting down through a block of silicone rubber and following exactly the line of a rifle held at the aim – along the top of the barrel and then, somehow, around the muzzle and back along the underside! And secondly, when the mould is reassembled and placed back in the mould box prior to casting, there are no locating lugs so its two halves can be slightly out of line. This means that when you cast your soldier, the centre line dividing back from front will form a tiny shelf because one half of your soldier will have shifted slightly to one side, or slightly higher than the other.

The answer is to make a two-piece mould. The mould you have just completed finished up as two pieces, because you cut it in half. But a two-piece mould begins that way: you set out to make one half, then a second half, and in the process you incorporate locating lugs which ensure that every time you cast, the mould's halves will be perfectly in line.

The First Half Begin by taking one of the thick end panels of your simple mould box, or the loose end panel of the improved box. Place this panel flat on your work surface and on its inside build up a block of Plasticine the same size as the panel – 90 mm x 100 mm – with neat, square edges. Some judgement is required when establishing the Plasticine's thickness. You want it to take up half the available space in the mould box; you know the box's short inside measurement is 80 mm; so your slab of Plasticine should be about 40 mm thick.

This slab of Plasticine forms – temporarily – one half of the mould, the other being formed from the first pouring of silicone rubber. You are going to push your soldier into it so that when the mould box is assembled his base will stand neatly on the box's plywood base, and the whole of his back half will be buried in Plasticine up to that familiar centre line along which you so carefully cut when making the one-piece mould – down through the centre of the ears, along the centre line of shoulder, centrally down the outside of the arm, leg, boot. When you have done that, and you assemble your mould box, your soldier will be standing in its centre. Behind him (from that centre line) there will be a slab of Plasticine the same size as the end panel, and 40 mm thick. In front of him there will be an empty space which you are going to fill with silicone rubber solution.

It should already be obvious why it's almost impossible to make a two-piece mould using a malleable master figure (I say 'almost' because someone, somewhere, will have found a way to do it). Indeed, it's quite difficult to push even a hard master figure into a solid block of Plasticine. The Plasticine needs to be quite warm and soft, and it helps to make a shallow depression prior to starting. Once the figure is in place you should use one of your shaping tools to create a sharp edge of Plasticine against the soldier's centre line. There must be no gaps through which the rubber solution can seep.

The alignment lugs mentioned earlier should be positioned on the flat surface close to the four corners of the Plasticine block. To make them you need an ordinary wooden pencil with a blunt point. Push this a little way into the Plasticine where alignment lugs are to be formed, leaving neat, conical holes.

Once you are satisfied with the soldier's position in the Plasticine, the sharpness of the Plasticine line where it touches him and the location of the alignment holes, assemble your box. Seal it as before with packing tape or an improved method you may have dreamed up. The edges of the Plasticine block may need trimming so that it fits neatly inside the box, and you should check that when the box is assembled the toy soldier's base is firmly against the base of the box. Once you are happy, work inside the box with your shaping tool (a little awkward, this) to seal the edges of the Plasticine block against the sides and base of the mould box – again, there should be no gaps.

This time when you prepare your silicone rubber and catalyst solution you will need only half the amount. Mix as before, pour slowly into a corner of the space in front of the soldier, and again stop once or twice to let any air bubbles float to the surface. When you have finished, put the mould box to one side to allow the first half of your mould to cure.

A metal soldier is here used to show the different stages in making a two-piece mould. The figure has been embedded in Plasticine, and a substantial strip of Plasticine laid round the figure

When the silicone rubber is fully cured, the mould box should be dismantled *with great care*. What you are setting out to do is to dismantle the box and remove the Plasticine from the toy soldier

Removing the Plasticine

The surrounding strip of Plasticine has now been moulded to the figure, with a clean edge formed where Plasticine and metal meet. Note the holes poked into the Plasticine, which will create alignment lugs in the completed silicone rubber mould

without disturbing his position in the silicone rubber.

If you are using a simple mould box this task is straightforward; all four sides can be gently peeled away. But whatever box you are using, once it has been dismantled you must keep the soldier pressed into the silicone rubber while peeling away the thick block of Plasticine – and, of course, all you can see or grasp is the soldier's base. Nevertheless, fingers are amazingly efficient tools. It is possible to grasp the block of silicone rubber, clear a little of the Plasticine away and use your thumb to hook around the soldier's base and, working from the bottom, gradually pull the Plasticine away. It gets easier. Once part of the soldier is exposed you can move your thumb further up his legs and hold him tightly against the silicone rubber.

If you are using the improved box, you must take more care at the outset. Remove the base, then slacken the wing nuts and take away the loose end panel, *leaving the Plasticine behind*. Remove the complete block of Plasticine and silicone rubber – with the soldier still sandwiched between them – from the opened box. It's probably easier to do this by sliding the block down rather than pulling it out through the opened end. Now remove the Plasticine, as explained above.

The Second Half   Plasticine can be annoyingly messy and, no matter how careful you are, silicone rubber tends to seep where it's not wanted. When you examine your toy soldier – with his front half buried claustrophobically in the block of silicone rubber and his back half exposed – you will find bits of Plasticine lodged in crevices and thin films of silicone rubber clinging to the curve of an arm or leg like shreds of skin. The bits of Plasticine should again be picked out with a sharp modelling tool and the unwanted silicone rubber sliced away with your craft knife so that the centre line around your soldier – now formed by silicone rubber – is once again clearly defined. Your paintbrush dipped in white spirit will also be needed.

Note the alignment lugs: those neat pencil holes poked into the Plasticine will have been filled by silicone rubber to form cones that now project from its surface.

Before beginning the second half of your mould by reassembling the mould box with the back of the silicone rubber block tight up against the end from which it was removed, one important bit of preparation is needed. A fresh silicone rubber solution poured in now would come up against an untreated silicone rubber surface and stick firmly to the half of the mould already formed. To prevent that happening you must mix a separating solution of white spirit and Vaseline and, using a fairly stiff paintbrush, apply this to the surface of the silicone rubber and to the exposed parts of the toy soldier. The ratio of white spirit to Vaseline is not all that important. If you fill an eggcup with white spirit, add something like a teaspoon of Vaseline and dissolve as much as you can with a thin mixing rod, that will do the job. Warming the white spirit helps the Vaseline dissolve, but *take great care* to ensure that you don't ignite the solution.

Alternatively, you can buy one of the release agents readily available – I have already mentioned Ambersil DP 100, which comes in a handy aerosol container and is easy to apply.

Right, all ready to go. Reassemble your box with the first half of the mould – complete with embedded soldier – back in position, and prepare your next batch of silicone rubber solution. Pour as before (this time into the space behind your toy soldier), pausing occasionally to get rid of air bubbles, then leave this second half of the mould to cure. And that's all there is to it.

Although a two-piece mould takes much longer to make than the simple one-piece (curing time alone is doubled), the process itself is full of interest and the end result most satisfying. When the final curing is complete and the mould box dismantled, you will find that the mould you have made splits neatly into its two halves (any unwanted rubber that has seeped across the join is easily cut away). Remove the master figure – it will still be in position nuzzling the first half of the mould – and put the two halves of the mould together; they will match beautifully, the alignment cones and holes mating perfectly to create a mould that will provide you with many perfect replicas of your 95th Rifleman.

Complicated Moulds

Master figures in complicated poses are easily reproduced by the two-piece mould method, and the methods used to produce a mould that will accommodate the more elaborate poses – and

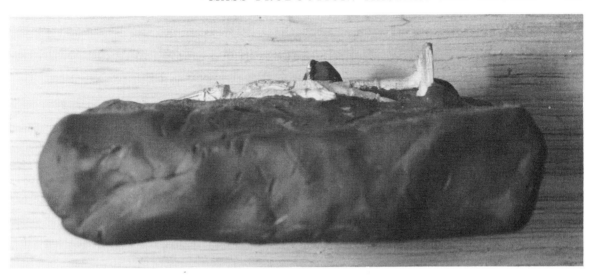

A side view of the embedded soldier, showing how the Plasticine has been built up beneath the extended left hand

still divide satisfactorily – are simply refinements of those described above.

Let's take one example. The obvious progression from your rifleman standing at attention would be to pose him in a marching position – left arm and right leg forward, right arm and left leg back (for the moment we'll ignore his musket). It's clear that if you now bury his back half in Plasticine, the familiar centre line is all right until we come down below his shoulders, then everything falls apart. The arm and leg pointing backwards have disappeared into the Plasticine block, while those pointing forwards are suspended in thin air.

In a case like this, what you do is continue to look at the same imaginary line down the *outside* of each arm and leg (even though it's changed position), and either cut back the Plasticine or build it up until the line is once again clearly defined. Do this while maintaining the 40 mm thickness of Plasticine at the edges of the block; you will have created small slopes leading up from this level to the leading arm and leg, small hollows leading down to the trailing limbs.

On the *inside* of the limbs, slope the Plasticine back from the inside of a projecting arm to the centre line down the side of the body, and back from the inside of a projecting leg to the centre line of the adjoining leg.

All this sounds terribly complicated, but when you actually place a master figure against a block of Plasticine it's amazing how clearly you can see the way the Plasticine needs to be manipulated.

The most complicated pose? Well, I would suggest a mounted

figure, in any position. You'll need a big mould box anyway, but the horse and rider must both be side on, the horse has four legs and … well, it's a nice problem for you to solve before we move on to the next stage, which is your first casting.

5 Mass Production: Casting

The toy soldier is traditionally cast in metal. Soldiers manufactured by Britains Ltd were hollow-cast, and many older readers will remember playing with toy armies whose casualties had their heads replaced by means of a broken matchstick jammed into head and body. Nowadays, toy soldiers and other figures for children are made of plastic, while toy soldiers produced for collectors – certainly those in Britain – are nearly all solid castings.

Metals used by modellers are alloys, typically containing tin, antimony and lead; tin and bismuth; or lead and bismuth. Pure bismuth can also be used, while lead-free pewter is made from tin, antimony and copper.

Simple castings can be made from plaster of Paris, while polyester and polyurethane resins are popular with makers of larger military miniatures. In such cases the entire figure can be made from resin, or the design can include parts made of a metal alloy. Both plaster of Paris and resin can be used to cast toy soldiers.

I will touch lightly on both these methods, but will concentrate on the production of a traditional toy soldier in a good-quality tin alloy.

- safety precautions
- preparing the mould

- using plaster of Paris
- casting in polyester resin
- hand pouring metal alloys
- makeshift centrifugal casting

Safety Precautions

Alloys of tin, antimony and lead suitable for casting toy soldiers will have a melting point of 243 degrees centigrade and a suggested operating temperature of around 300 degrees centigrade. Severe injury can be caused if these metals are handled carelessly, and they will virtually explode if the merest droplet of water is allowed to come into contact with them. So at the very least you should consider using goggles and leather gloves. There is unlikely to be a health risk from any metal alloy except those rich in lead; warnings will be clearly marked on containers or packaging.

Polyester resins are toxic and have a low flashpoint. When using them, adequate ventilation is essential, and if you are considering casting with resin you are strongly advised to consult the advice on safety available from suppliers. Briefly, this deals with precautions relating to skin and eye care and emphasizes that absolute cleanliness is necessary: disposable aprons and overalls should be used to protect clothing, polythene sheets to cover benches. If in any doubt about the adequacy of ventilation you can easily get hold of facemasks designed to protect against organic vapours like those given off by polyester resin.

Preparing the Mould

If you take your mould, divide it into its two halves and examine the concavities that are the negative images of your toy soldier, you will see at once that to get metal into it you are going to have to cut an opening somewhere. Earlier I suggested that you design the mould so that your soldier's base is standing firmly on the plywood base of the mould box. This was done deliberately, because I have discovered by trial and error that it's the only sure way of casting a base that will be free from distortion.

The position of your soldier in the mould leads to another conclusion: the opening through which you are going to pour the metal alloy can lead into either your soldier's head (or hat) or the base. Let's look at both possibilities.

If you put the two halves of your mould together again and turn it upside down, you will see the broad, open area that is the base and in it two holes: the soldier's feet. These are perfect, ready-made pouring holes, and apart from the minor difficulties of getting the metal into areas such as the tips of fingers (which are pointing against the flow), hand pouring – or drop-casting – in this way is perfectly feasible. The only other slight but obvious problem is that when the metal cools the underside of the base will be rounded, and will need to be ground flat during the finishing process. The main advantage is that the base contains the only existing opening into your mould, and if you use that as a pouring hole there are no openings left to seal.

Now let's look at the other method, cutting a pouring hole at the top of the mould. I have always drop-cast in this way, and I have done so for two main reasons. First, a toy soldier's hands and arms almost always point downwards to a greater or lesser degree, so by pouring alloy through the soldier's head the flow will be down the arms to the fingertips. And secondly, because the figure's base will be flat against the base of the mould box, its underside will be perfectly smooth and will require no finishing work.

For those two reasons I recommend this method, and to proceed you will need to cut an opening through the top of the mould using a sharp craft knife. Place one half of the mould flat on your work surface and, beginning at the centre/top of your rifleman's hat, make a shallow cut back towards the top edge of the mould at an angle of about 60 degrees. Do the same in the opposite direction so that you have marked out an inverted triangle, its apex at the top of your soldier's hat, its base at the mould's top edge.

This triangle is the outline of the pouring hole, which should now be carefully cut in the shape of a smooth half cone. When the other half of the mould has been treated in the same way and the two halves are brought together a neat, conical hole will be formed, at whose inner apex – the centre of the soldier's hat – an opening perhaps 2 mm in diameter will permit molten metal to enter the mould.

When metal pours into the mould, air must come out – and it can't come out through that tiny entry hole. So the next step is to cut air vents, channels or 'sprues'. Cut the main vents from each end of the soldier's base – a single channel cut into the flat mould surface, on either side of the figure, that will carry air from the base to the top edge of the mould on either side of the pouring hole (but a comfortable distance away from it – perhaps midway between it and the side edge of the mould). If you haven't got a special sprue cutter, use your craft knife again and make these channels a couple of millimetres wide and deep.

If you were to assemble your mould now and pour in metal alloy at the correct temperature, you would probably cast a

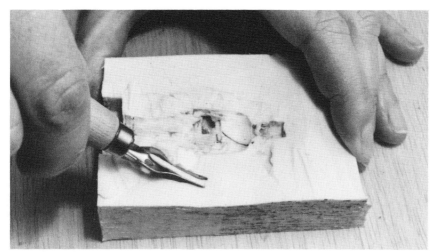

With the mould in two halves, airways or sprues can be cut. Here a special tool is being used, but a sharp craft knife will work just as well

figure that looked fine, but had one or two imperfections. This almost always happens with a first cast – even into a perfectly prepared mould – because the molten metal hits cold silicone rubber and cools too quickly. But the most probable cause in the case of a mould that is still being prepared is that air has been trapped somewhere.

When hand pouring, the metal moves downwards under the effect of gravity. If you can imagine a mould made from a master figure whose arms are slightly away from its body, but still pointing downwards, you can see that the cavities will be perfect dead ends; the metal will pour down them, and be stopped by a trapped cushion of air somewhere down near the hands. In such cases you must cut more air vents, so that the metal is able to flow freely to the very tips of the fingers.

Because the 95th Rifleman is of simple design, the only likely air traps are in the fingers and thumb of the right hand, which I suggested you leave open so that the Baker rifle can be grasped. However, just to make things even, assume that the clenched left fist will be another air trap, and from both those potential dead ends cut narrow air vents leading to the main air vents you have already cut up each side. Cut these new vents so that they slope gently upwards. If you sloped them the other way, metal would flow down the arms into the hands, then continue on down the narrow air vents.

Using Plaster of Paris

Although I have been talking about metal, the mould you have prepared can be filled with a number of compounds. The simplest, and arguably the safest, is plaster of Paris. There are

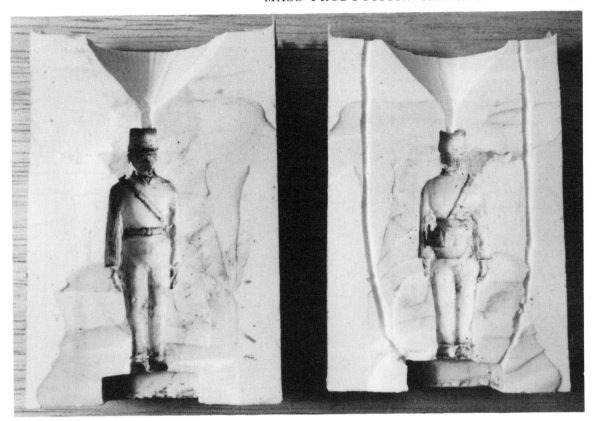

The two halves of the mould, showing the negative impression of the master figure, and the freshly cut sprues. When the halves are brought together in the mould box, white metal will be poured into the conical hole at the top. The two airways will permit metal to fill the base

several varieties, some being for general use while others have been produced for a specific purpose like dental work. Most are inexpensive. To use, the plaster is mixed gently into the required amount of water: for general plasters the ratio of plaster to water can range from 1¾lb: pint to more than 4lb: pint. Setting time is somewhere between 10 minutes and half an hour. Plasters can be surprisingly hard, and when water is replaced by plaster polymer that hardness increases dramatically.

You will need:

- the mould
- the mould box
- plaster of Paris
- clean water
- a mixing bowl and spatula
- a plaster brush

When working at this scale, plaster is suitable only for very simple figures. I've never used it for toy soldiers, but I've watched my son cast a delightful Mexican figure in a silicone rubber mould. It must have been about 75 or 100 mm high, and it stood for years in a large plant pot in the garden, getting some shelter from a small shrub but inevitably battered by wind and rain.

You might just manage to cast your 95th Rifleman in plaster. Use the spatula to mix the plaster into the water in your mixing bowl. The amount of water can be adjusted, and I would suggest that if you want to try, use a mixture as thin as you can make it. For convenience, put the mould in its mould box, and make sure it's secure. The only precautions you need take are to ensure that the base of the box is held tight against the bottom of the mould. Once you have filled the mould, tap it gently on the work surface a couple of times to help the liquid plaster settle into the smaller crevices.

A refinement of this technique is to mix the plaster before assembling the mould, and brush some of the liquid plaster into the mould cavity so that those small crevices are pre-filled. It's the same principle you used when brushing the silicone rubber solution on the outside of your master figure before pouring the mould.

Accessories such as weapons will need to be made from something other than plaster. The finished plaster model will be feather-light and a delight to behold, its surface smooth and white, and warm to the touch. Needless to say, these delicate models must always be handled with care. I have one final suggestion before we move on. When you assemble the mould prior to pouring the plaster, put a small weight (fishermen's lead shot is ideal) in the base. This will be held tightly by the plaster, put additional weight where it's needed and help your sturdy plaster soldier to stay on his feet!

Casting in Polyester Resin

You will need to have access to the following:

- mould
- mould box
- resin
- catalyst
- mixing cup
- brushes
- metal filler

Polyester resin can be cast with great success in a silicone rubber mould, and although handling the resin and catalyst can be a fairly complicated and messy procedure, some of the techniques suggested above will prove useful. I'm not going to give any instruction on the preparation and mixing of polyester resin and catalyst (liquid hardener), because the supplier's instructions are usually comprehensive and will tell you all you need to know. Indeed, suppliers such as Alec Tiranti have excellent booklets for sale that provide a vast amount of detailed information and guide you step by step through the various working methods.

Once the resin has been prepared you can again use the technique of brushing a thin film of the mixture into the two halves of the mould. The resin should have a comfortable brushing consistency, and should be kept away from those surfaces of the mould that will be brought together. When you have finished brushing – paying particular attention to fine detail and undercuts – put the two halves of the mould into the mould box, secure, and fill the mould with catalysed resin. It should now be set aside to cure.

That describes resin casting at its simplest. It is ideal for the production of light, strong toy soldiers of simple design that will be painted and eventually take their place in the ranks. But before leaving resin casting I must briefly mention the technique of casting with catalysed resin mixed with metal powder, which enables the modeller to produce miniature soldiers – in resin/bronze, for example – that are virtually indistinguishable from conventionally cast bronzes.

The mixture to be brushed into the mould is made up from catalysed resin and a bronze filler powder (or another metal of your choice); it is applied to the inside of the mould as described above. But this time the two halves are kept apart and set aside to cure. The mixture used to fill the mould, with its two shells, when the two halves are brought together consists of resin and an inert filler (which is less expensive than metal powder). When this second resin mix has been allowed to cure and the toy soldier is removed from the mould you will have a solid figure made of resin and an inert filler, covered with a thin, hard skin of resin impregnated with bronze.

The surface should now be worked with fine wire wool, then polished with a burnishing cream or a good metal polish.

Both the methods briefly described above work well with small figures – and you won't come across figures much smaller than a 54-mm toy soldier! If resin casting does appeal to you, you are more likely to be attracted by the first method, which will give you figures that are a delight to paint. The technique of casting with resin and a metal powder is more suitable for the production of soldiers that are, perhaps, to be mounted on a wooden base and displayed individually.

To make your first cast in the prepared mould you will need:

Hand-pouring Tin Alloy

- the mould
- the mould box
- tin alloy
- ladle
- talcum or graphite powder
- a heat source
- goggles (or protective glasses)
- gloves
- a shallow metal tray.

At this stage of modelling toy soldiers you will almost certainly move your bits and pieces into the kitchen. My wife could relate hair-raising tales about our cottage in North Wales, whose small kitchen had a glittering circle of tin alloy around the walls, just above the skirting board. This was from my early Heath Robinson attempts at centrifugal casting (of which more later), but you can confidently reassure whoever shares your home that casting by hand is a relatively tidy process.

You will require only a small quantity of tin alloy, and the easiest way to melt it is to use a flat-bottomed ladle that, when filled with metal pieces, will stand unsupported on the heat source – a gas or electric stove is ideal (hence the kitchen).

The final bit of preparation before assembling your mould in its box is to dust the cavities in each half with either graphite powder or talcum powder. By creating an interface between metal and mould, the powder tends to improve the quality of the casting. I prefer talcum powder. Graphite powder is quite expensive and blackens everything it touches, whereas every house will have a tin of talc in the bathroom – Johnson's Baby Powder is ideal – and of course it's very clean.

When you've applied the powder, bang the backs of the mould halves to get rid of any excess, then bring their inner faces together (mating the alignment lugs and holes) and secure the assembled mould in your mould box. Once again, your main concern when sealing is to ensure that the base of the box is tight against the base of the mould (strong elastic bands are ideal). Now stand the mould box in the metal tray to catch any spillage and melt the tin alloy over the heat source. It's wise to don your leather gloves before starting.

A flat ladle ideal for hand-pouring molten white metal

In the section on safety precautions (p.62) I quoted tin/lead/antimony alloys as having a melting temperature of 243 degrees centigrade and a recommended operating temperature of about 300 degrees centigrade. But there is an excellent alloy consisting of lead and bismuth (no tin) which melts at 168 degrees centigrade, has a working temperature of around 225 degrees centigrade, and is ideal for producing figures by the hand-pouring method. It is the No.4 Low Melt Alloy available from Alec Tiranti Ltd, of London and Theale, and I suggest you use this metal for your early attempts, because it is very similar to one I used when I was experiencing casting problems.

Recommended temperatures aren't really of much help, because this is a primitive method of casting and you are going to be using judgement, not a thermometer. The aim is to pour the alloy into the mould at the lowest possible temperature that will still give good metal flow. The procedure is simple: put on your protective glasses, watch the alloy heating in the ladle and, when it is completely liquid, carry it to your mould and pour it in one smooth motion directly into the conical opening.

You will be surprised, as I was, at the small amount of metal needed to fill the mould. It seems that no sooner have you started pouring than the metal wells up to the top of the pouring hole. Nevertheless, almost certainly your mould is full, and you should now set it to one side for a minute or so while the metal solidifies. Then dismantle your mould box and, holding the mould in your gloved hand with one half uppermost, gently work this away from the freshly cast figure.

Two important points. First, if you become impatient and split the mould too soon, you will find bits of soft metal coming away with the mould and the soldier will be ruined. And, secondly, if you do manage to curb your impatience and wait long enough for the metal to solidify, take care when splitting the mould. If you pull it away too quickly, silicone rubber tucked behind undercuts may tear, ruining the mould.

This is a moment that, to me at any rate, never loses its excitement. True, there is a feeling of great satisfaction when an original figure worked in one or other of the modelling compounds is finished, but somehow the sense of sheer wonder doesn't come until that first metal figure is cast. Perhaps it's because a figure cast in tin alloy (not bismuth) is so bright and shiny; in one simple action the original figure with its bits tacked on and its dull, matt surface of many different shades has been transformed, and in truth you are seeing it for the first time. Perhaps it's the sheer speed of the process that amazes; your original took you several days, this simple cast a matter of seconds. Or perhaps it's because, suddenly, you realize that you have before you the means of producing countless identical figures, with virtually no effort.

For whatever reason, this is a moment to cherish – but when you've luxuriated in that moment take a deep breath, cast aside the excitement, look critically at your casting and come down to earth with a bump! Yes, as I mentioned earlier, there will be imperfections. Certainly you will need to make a second cast into the now warm mould, because even if there are no bits obviously missing from your soldier the fine detail will be blurred, edges that should be sharp will be rounded and a Roman or aquiline nose will be noticeably snub.

If there are any missing parts, see if the reason is because the air vents are inadequate, or wrongly located. There should be no such problems with your 95th Rifleman, but other figures you design might, for example, have hats with wide, thin brims. Getting metal to flow into these is always difficult, and you will almost certainly need an air vent leading from each side of the brim. Muskets or rifles held at the aim will need an air vent leading from their muzzles; plumes or cockades that stand above the hat will need vents leading directly to the mould's upper edge.

Close examination of the figure and mould (plus lots of practice) will soon show you what needs to be done to cure casting faults. And with a well-designed mould that is correctly vented and has been warmed by a couple of preliminary casts

The first casting has been made, and the two halves of the mould separated. Note how the metal has begun to flow up the right hand airway; the flash on the bottom and left hand side of the base; and the nodule on the tail of the soldier's jacket, formed by an air bubble in the mould

you will, with careful handling, be able to produce one perfect figure after another – an army of toy soldiers.

Makeshift Centrifugal Casting

Pouring a few grams of metal into a mould 90 mm high and expecting gravity to fill every nook and cranny might smack of optimism. That it works so well is a tribute to the manufacturers of the materials you use and, of course, your own skill in preparing the mould – in particular the way you cut airways so that the metal flows as freely as possible.

But for extra crispness, and to ensure that the most awkward areas in complicated moulds are filled, something more than gravity is needed, and it was this necessity that led inventive minds to centrifugal casting. I intend to cover this process more fully in a later chapter, but it's worth touching on now because I know modellers love experimenting – which is exactly what I did when I began making toy soldiers. I wanted to cast centrifugally and began to look around for ways and means.

At that time I had a very old swivel chair. It was a heavy contraption with three thick wooden legs curving in and up to a central point – rather like those on an old-fashioned umbrella stand. The chair itself was mounted on top of those legs on a platform resting on a marvellous ball race. I removed the chair and mounted a circular board on top of the ball race. That gave me a flat surface, mounted on solid legs, that could be spun by hand. I now arranged to fix my mould box – on its side – at the edge of the mounting board, with the pouring hole pointing towards the centre. For balance when spinning, a counterweight was secured on the edge of the board directly opposite.

A quick digression now to explain centrifugal casting. Everyone knows what happens in a spin-drier. Put the clothes in, press the start button and as the drum spins the clothes are thrown from the centre and held against the drum walls. Centrifugal casting works on exactly the same principle. If you pour water into the centre of a spin-drier, it will be flung to the sides; pour metal into a centrifugal casting machine, and it gets thrown outwards, ideally into all those awkward nooks and crannies.

My system gave me something that could be spun by hand. If a small wooden box were placed against the wall inside a spin-drier with its open end towards the centre, during spinning, water would be thrown into the box. My box was mounted on what was essentially a hand-operated spin-drier without the walls. All I needed was a means of directing the molten metal into the mould box, and I had a workable system.

What I did was take an old metal cup I'd won when I was a cross-country runner, removed the elegant base, drilled a hole in the bottom of the cup, cut a hole near the rim and fixed a blanking plate across the cup's circular top. I was left with a cone-shaped metal container with a hole at the apex that could be fixed against the mould's pouring hole and an opening at the wide end through which metal could be poured. To use this amazingly primitive system I simply assembled the mould and mould box with the apex of the metal cup tight up against the mould's pouring hole, fixed them in position on the mounting board, melted the metal, poured it into the modified running trophy and instantly spun my casting machine by hand.

And it worked. I kept the machine spinning for about thirty seconds or so to allow the metal to solidify, then let it slow and stop. When the mould was dismantled the metal had been thrown into the mould and the tiniest crevice filled under a force somewhat greater than that of gravity. Castings were pin sharp.

The amount of metal melted was purposely more than was required to cast a 54-mm toy soldier, so when the mould was dismantled the soldier was left with the modified trophy fixed solidly to his hat by the solid lump of excess metal. That was simply snipped off. The whole process was slow but, primitive or not, it was effective centrifugal casting.

My contraption was liable, as previously mentioned, to expel (with a nasty hissing sound) a quantity of molten metal that formed a neat border of white metal around the kitchen walls if something on the mould box happened to break loose. As the device was operated manually – by me – then at such times I would suddenly develop a neat line of glittering white metal across the front of my trousers, just below each knee. The trousers were always ruined; the red blotches on my skin faded, but with painful slowness. The lesson, of course, is that although I'm talking light-heartedly about crazy experiments that, in a funny sort of way, actually worked, molten metal is dangerous and should always be treated with respect.

I've heard it said that centrifugal casting in toy soldier terms was developed when an enterprising modeller decided that there was a less obvious but more exciting use for an old record turntable. Can you imagine that scene? An old-fashioned record-player on the kitchen table, wire trailing across the stove to a wall socket, the turntable spinning and, bent over it, a man wearing thick protective glasses pouring molten metal into … Well, into the mould, eventually – but what he'd jury- rigged in between is anybody's guess.

The front view of the completed metal toy soldier. The base has been cleaned up, and the musket glued to the right hand. Here it can be seen that the toy soldier is extremely simple, and it is interesting to compare this casting with the painted version

6 Finishing

I have waxed lyrical about the appearance of that first casting when it emerges from the mould, and will stoutly defend my words in the face of all opposition: the first casting made from each original figure you design is always exciting, and it's such moments that make modelling toy soldiers both enjoyable and fascinating.

However … you now have in your hands a metal toy soldier, but he is still a long way from being complete, spick and span, and ready to march proudly onto the parade ground. Close examination of every casting, for instance, will reveal markings that are a natural result of the casting process, and before any progress can be made towards the figure's completion these must be removed.

Examination of the casting also serves another purpose. The mould may have suffered from excessive heat or rough handling, and now is the best time to pinpoint any damage.

Once the casting has been thoroughly cleaned it is often possible to adjust the pose, and even if that's not necessary or desirable most figures will have weapons that have been cast separately, and must now be attached. However, because your assembly strategy will in part be determined by the problems associated with painting, read the later section in this chapter, entitled 'Completion' (p.77), in conjunction with the beginning of Chapter 7.

73

This chapter covers:

- cleaning the casting – checking the mould
- animating
- soldering – and the alternatives
- completion
- refinements

Cleaning the Casting – Checking the Mould

It is a good idea to wash the toy soldier in hot water and detergent as soon as it is removed from the mould. But before doing so, examine it closely, looking in particular at any undercuts. If you find tiny bits of silicone rubber lodged in such places you will know that there has been some damage to the mould. This shouldn't happen if care has been taken in removing the soldier (although it does become more likely as the mould ages with each casting), but it's annoying to know that small pieces torn from the mould cause more trouble than major damage.

When a tiny piece of rubber is torn away by becoming trapped in an undercut – let's say it's in the cavity between a soldier's chin and his sharp collar – in all subsequent castings that undercut will be filled by solid metal the same shape as the piece of missing rubber. This unwanted metal must somehow be cut or drilled away to restore the original shape of the chin and collar, and when working with metal it takes time, and in particularly awkward spots can be virtually impossible.

There is also little use in trying to cure future problems by sticking back such tiny fragments of rubber into the mould. Special adhesives are readily available, but these tiny pieces are so irregularly shaped that getting them back where they were the right way round is more trouble than it's worth. On the other hand large rips in the mould, or chunks that have become detached, are usually easily repaired, so at this stage make a note of the damage and put the mould to one side to be worked on later.

Flash

Your mould is in two halves and during casting those two halves are pressed tightly together within the constraints of the mould box. If they are not, hot molten metal will seep between the halves. With a good mould box, a well-prepared mould and careful casting, that seepage is stopped completely, and all you will see is a fine hairline around the toy soldier marking where the mould splits. In the worst cases, your soldier will emerge with a thin metal shim – known as 'flash' – all around him, firmly attached to that dividing line down both sides of his head, arms, body and legs.

When that occurs you will need to cut away the flash with a sharp craft knife, being careful not to damage the figure. Then remove all traces of either that excessive flashing, or the fine mould line, with a smooth file followed by emery cloth or paper.

Sprues A sprue refers to the channel through which you poured metal into the mould, the metal that has solidified in that channel, and the various air passages. When you split the mould you are going to find a conical sprue attached to your 95th Rifleman's hat and there will be other sprues that solidified in the airways you cut to improve metal flow. Two will be attached to the corners of the base and two to the soldier's hands. All of these should be snipped or cut away – with a craft knife if they are thin, with metal cutters if they are more substantial – and again the area cleaned up with a file and emery cloth.

Animating It is always best to arrive at the correct or most attractive pose during the early modelling work, because subsequent excessive bending of the arms, for example, will mean that a V-shaped cut must be made in the hollow of the elbow. Such drastic reshaping should certainly be done when working on the master figure.

Very little can be done to your 95th Rifleman to adjust his pose – which, at its simplest, is what is meant by animation – but you will inevitably progress to modelling figures that, even at such a late stage, can be bent and shaped reasonably freely.

Most adjustment still possible on a final casting will be to the arms; a toy soldier's feet are fixed firmly to the base, which rules out any leg movement. Arms, however, can be bent slightly, moved towards or away from the body; hands can sometimes be opened or closed, or their angle adjusted in relation to the wrist; and occasionally, if there is no heavy collar, the head can be tilted or even turned a little to improve the soldier's appearance.

Most adjustments to a finished casting will be to correct slight misalignment, or to facilitate the fitting of weapons or other accoutrements, and this is exactly what must be done to the rifleman. Earlier, I recommended that his right hand be left slightly open – thumb away from the finger mass – so that at a later stage he could grasp the Baker rifle. That stage has now been reached, and when we have discussed the ways and means of affixing bits and bobs to toy soldiers, he must be suitably and permanently armed.

For those of you who know nothing about soldering, the basic procedure is to apply a very small quantity of melted metal – solder – to the parts to be joined, using a special soldering iron. To do this effectively, both parts to be joined must be warmed sufficiently for the solder to flow freely. With two metal parts of approximately equal size and a suitable flux – a liquid or paste that is applied to help the metals flow and fuse – there is no problem.

Unfortunately, a solid toy soldier contains an awesome mass of metal when compared with a rifle or musket in the same scale, and if a normal soldering iron is used in conjunction with a standard solder that slender little rifle would melt into a shapeless blob before the soldier had begun to warm. Nevertheless, soldering of one kind or another is probably the best way of joining two metals, and so the boffins have done their stuff and come up with the perfect answer.

The technique involves the use of a controlled soldering iron that can be set to a chosen temperature within the range 128 to 400 degrees centigrade. The iron is used in conjunction with a special low-melt solder containing lead, bismuth, cadmium and tin. The parts to be joined are painted with a water-based flux, then, using the controlled iron at the correct temperature, coated with a thin film of low-melt solder. Finally, the two parts are brought together, heat is again applied and, as the solder on the two parts mingles and is left to cool, a strong joint is formed. The joint can be washed clean with water.

Normal safety precautions apply. Even a controlled soldering iron can be quite hot, so a safety stand should be used to hold the iron when not in use. Low-melt solder contains cadmium. It should not be overheated, as cadmium is a highly toxic metal and at high temperatures the fumes given off are harmful.

Soldering – and the Alternatives
Soldering

Many military modellers, and professional manufacturers, assemble their kits or add the bits and pieces needed to complete a toy soldier using one or other of the excellent adhesives now available.

Holding separate pieces tightly together while a glue sets has always been a problem, and many applications and adhesives require complicated clamping arrangements. The problem with toy soldiers is that the parts are extremely small, so anything that speeds up the process without sacrificing strength is an obvious boon. Superglues come into that category, and are now used regularly.

Superglues have other advantages. Two-part epoxy glues such

Adhesives

as Araldite or Araldite Rapid are excellent, but they are sticky and when used to fix parts to toy soldiers tend to leave fine threads of glue where they're not wanted, and a hard excess around the joined parts that must be sliced away. As well as setting almost instantaneously, the superglues are liquid and colourless, and an infinitesimal quantity is all that's needed to effect a good bond. They leave no sticky threads or unwanted lumps that need to be painstakingly removed.

Disadvantages? Well, I have heard that in time the lead in a toy soldier reacts with the superglue and breaks down the adhesion – but nobody has yet been able to tell me if that is a fact, or if it is, how long the joint takes to deteriorate and fall apart. When the pros and cons are weighed up, it's probably a risk worth taking.

There are contact adhesives such as Bostik that are applied to the parts to be joined, then left until dry to the touch, at which point the two parts are brought together – correctly positioned! Others, such as Copydex, will join fabrics. You will choose the best one for the purpose and, like most modellers, you will find that a toy soldier marches the long road to perfection along a variety of different routes.

Completion

With your first 95th Rifleman casting cleaned up, mould part lines removed and sprue attachment points smoothed so that it seems they never existed, you are ready to arm him with the two weapons you cast separately: the Baker rifle and the sword bayonet.

With the Baker rifle, you have two alternative positions. Earlier in this book I suggested that because the rifleman has been designed and cast standing in a kind of modified 'attention' position, the rifle would eventually be held in the soldier's right hand, the butt resting alongside his right foot. If that position suits you, then all that's needed now is to put a dab of adhesive against the inside of the butt, the outside of the foot, and on the inside of his right hand. Then place the Baker rifle in position. The upper part of the rifle barrel rests between thumb and fingers, and with a pair of snipe-nose pliers these should be gently closed. At this scale the hand is too small actually to grip the rifle, but the adhesive will hold the rifle in the correct position to create a passable illusion.

The alternative is to fix the rifle to your soldier as if he is holding it vertically against his right side with his index finger

A side view of the assembled casting

through the trigger guard. That sounds as if some intricate modelling work is needed to drill a hole in the trigger guard and manipulate the hand, but because we are dealing with a toy soldier it can be quite simple. This time the hand – fingers and thumb – will be outside the rifle, directly alongside the trigger guard. If you want to aim for perfection, use a small file to remove the top half of the index finger, so that it appears to be inserted into the trigger guard; you should certainly bend the thumb so that it touches the rifle sling close to the lower sling swivel. Adhesive will again go on the inside of the hand, and you might think it worthwhile putting a dab on the butt where it touches the leg.

If you have been following the illustration in *British Infantry Equipment 1808–1908* you will have noted that the sword bayonet is carried on the soldier's left side in a frog suspended from the waist belt. Because the rifleman is in the attention position, if you modelled the frog at all you will have positioned it behind his left arm. All that's required now is to put a dab of adhesive on the back of the sword bayonet – just below the hilt – and fix it in the correct position against the bayonet frog.

Incidentally, one way of fudging or getting around bits you don't feel confident of handling is to model them *covered* by an arm. If, for instance, instead of casting a separate bayonet you had modelled it as a solid piece running down the side of the rifleman's left thigh – with his hand resting on it as if he were holding it – this trick would enable you to hide the bayonet hilt, and create a realistic pose. (In all of the above, read 'solder' for 'adhesive' if you prefer to work that way.)

Refinements

Modelling of any kind is a very personal pursuit, and what satisfies one craftsman will to another look like a job half completed. In this final assembly work, and in the painting that follows, there is always scope for imaginative improvements, and even a figure in the simple pose we have chosen is no exception.

Another position for the Baker rifle is slung over the right shoulder. To achieve this you will need to make a sling from shim metal – or perhaps that lead wire I mentioned earlier (page 39) – and glue or solder it to the rifle's sling swivels. Once the rifle is in position behind the shoulder the hand will again be glued outside the trigger guard, but this time the rifle will come inside the hand from the rear. (Depending on how you designed the right hand, you may need to do some judicious cutting with a craft knife or junior hacksaw.) His thumb will now rest inside

Examples of toy soldier
weapons and accessories.
Two of those on the right
still have bits of sprue
attached

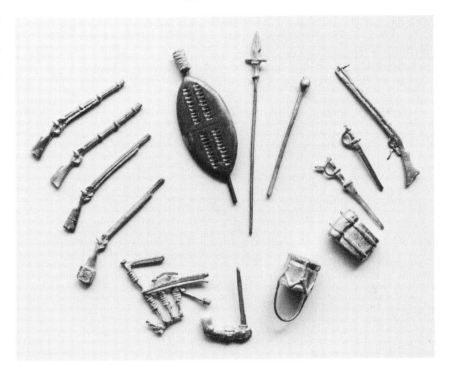

the sling, against the lower sling swivel.

The rifleman's hackle is the fluffy bit that sits above the cockade at the top/front of his hat. A tiny piece of pipe cleaner, dyed green and glued in position, will add startling realism.

Fine green thread of the kind used for embroidery can be used to represent the cord holding the powder flask. Lay it along the centre of the whole length of the pouch belt – tiny, spaced dabs of glue will hold it secure and suggest the tubes through which the cord was threaded – and where the cord leaves the back of the pouch belt to be secured to the powder flask it will look very effective.

An effective refinement is achieved by glueing fine sawdust to the upper surface of the soldier's integral base. At the painting stage suitable colours can be chosen so that it represents sand, dark soil or grass. Although these bases are small, there is even room to fix tiny pebbles (and I do mean tiny).

Finally, if you really want to create a small display or diorama, fillers such as Tetrion can be used as a groundwork into which several soldiers' bases can be pressed so that their tops are flush with the Tetrion. Scattering sawdust will completely disguise the sunken bases and, when coloured, again create the illusion of rough terrain. By letting your imagination soar you will come up with broken cartwheels ('borrowed' from your son's farmyard toys), trees splintered by cannonballs (a twig torn from a bush) and ...

But, hold on a second, we seem to have drifted a long way beyond the modelling of a simple toy soldier, and it really is time we got back on track.

7 Painting

Toy soldiers are invariably finished using high-gloss paints, and it is this particular feature that many collectors find so attractive. Opponents of this type of painting would argue that the nature of the finish means that it is impossible to incorporate many of the subtle refinements found in connoisseur figures; they are generally painted using oil paints, matt enamels or acrylic colours, and outstanding realism can be achieved through the clever use of shading and highlighting. But my own opinion is that if a figure is well designed there is no need to use skilful brushwork to adjust light and shade. The curves and hollows formed by the figure's shape and its carefully contrived pose will create natural shadows and highlights, and gloss paints emphasize both with matchless brilliance.

However, because gloss enamels can be tricky to handle, and dry slowly, I am going to look at other finishes and discuss techniques that produce results that are at least as good as those achieved with gloss paints.

Apart from the natural beauty of gloss paints, they have other advantages. Gloss-painted figures can be handled without fear of leaving unsightly grease marks. Dust doesn't settle on them so heavily – or at least it doesn't appear to – and is more easily removed. And although I can't quote from statistics, my own feeling is that gloss paints last longer, with very little deterioration in the quality of the finish.

Toy soldiers need care, of course, and we will be discussing that in detail in Chapter 8. In this chapter we will be looking at:

- priming and preparation
- brushes, airbrushes and aerosols
- selecting and mixing colours
- working to a system
- general painting techniques
- adding essential detail
- advanced painting techniques

Priming and Preparation

In Chapter 6 I told you in some detail how you should assemble your toy soldier, but mentioned also that you should read those instructions in conjunction with sections from this chapter. The reason is that quite often it's better to leave the final assembly until you have finished painting. If you are going to tuck a Baker rifle tight up against your soldier's uniform, one or the other is going to suffer in the painting – and some sections of the barrel and trigger guard will be impossible to reach.

You will come across this problem more frequently when you begin to design soldiers in awkward poses, or with masses of bulky equipment that mean parts must be cast separately. So, backtracking just a little, the first part of your painting preparation comes just before you begin to assemble the completed figure. Place the loose bits such as packs, blanket rolls and, yes, rifles and bayonets in the position where they will be glued or soldered, and see if it's possible to get a brush behind them – and if you are able to see what you are doing when it's there. If you can't – either reach or see – then leave that bit of equipment off and paint it separately.

The main preparation for painting is the application of a suitable primer. When I began making toy soldiers I used to brush each figure with a thinned coat of Humbrol matt grey – there are several shades, and I used the lightest. When my production increased I began to apply the same undercoat with an airbrush, but the mixture had to be exactly right, and still the nozzle tended to clog. Finally, I turned to the motor factors and bought an aerosol can of white primer, and since then I have used nothing else. No brush marks, no clogging and, depending on the brand you use (because they do vary), a wonderful smooth coating on which it is a pleasure to paint.

Just two points about these white aerosols. Remember that you need plenty of ventilation when using them, and if there is any doubt, use a mask. And don't spray indiscriminately; the mist drifts everywhere, and you will find yourself dusting a white deposit off everything from the kitchen stove to the grand piano.

**Brushes,
Airbrushes and
Aerosols**
Brushes

When working on a 54-mm figure you will need paintbrushes that apply broad masses of colour, and others that are fine enough to paint dots smaller than the head of a pin and lines that can be as fine as a hair. And as with all kinds of painting, going for cheapness is not only a false economy, it produces poor results.

I have always used Rowney S34 Sable brushes. Size 0 is ideal for those fine details, and sizes 2 or 3 are as large as you need go for painting larger areas such as jackets, trousers and bases. In fact, such is the quality of these brushes that as long as they are kept in good condition even the larger sizes can be used for surprisingly fine detail. Winsor & Newton's Series 33 School of Art Sable are also excellent, and if treated with care all of these brushes will give long service. Clean them well in white spirit after every use, and it's a good idea to dip them in washing-up liquid and bring them to a fine point before putting them away for the night (don't forget to rinse them the next time you begin painting!).

There are also brushes on the market that make use of artificial fibres. I have tried them, but was unimpressed. However, they are less expensive, and you may find that they suit your style of painting.

Airbrushes

Toy soldiers are so small that it seems pointless even mentioning airbrushes. But you will recall that I once used an airbrush for applying an undercoat or primer, and as well as that particular use there are other tasks that can be handled reasonably well by these versatile tools.

I'm thinking in particular of the time when you will have a lot of identical figures to paint. Your 95th Riflemen wear green jackets, and if you have cast two dozen or so it's quite feasible to stand them in a line, load an airbrush reservoir with suitably thinned paint and go along the line airbrushing the jackets. There is a good, wide dividing line between jackets and trousers – the waist belt. Use an index card to mask the legs, holding it close to the soldier with *its upper edge just below the upper edge of the belt*. You can use your airbrush to put a beautiful coat of paint on the jacket, and leave a neat line along the belt. Don't bother to mask the face. One of the beauties of gloss paints is that they cover well, and when the green has dried you will have no problems over-painting flesh or any other colour.

A typical hobbyist's work bench, with the 95th Rifleman. Painting is in progress, and the Rifleman is nearing completion

Before you jump on me, yes, I do realize that when using this method the soldier's arms can create problems. If he is posed with his arms away from his body it's not too bad; the masking card can be slipped between arms and body, leaving the arms entirely exposed to the paint spray. However, if there is no gap between the arms and body then when you place your masking cardboard along the waistbelt you are going to cover the lower portion of the arms, which will get no paint. And to that quandary, of course, there is only one answer: those small sections must be painted with a brush (but not just yet, as you will see in a moment).

When the jackets have been painted – and are still wet – you can use your airbrush to paint the grey trousers. Again use the waistbelt as the dividing line, this time masking the upper half of the soldier by holding the index card with *its bottom edge a little above the lower edge of the belt, taking care not to let it touch the figure.* When the trousers have been sprayed, each soldier will be left with a waist belt that is green at the top and grey at the bottom – and you have saved a lot of time as well as avoiding unsightly brush marks. Apart, that is, from another problem with the arms: this time they will have been painted, but the wrong colour. Solution: let them dry, and now, at last, you can use your brush to paint them to match the rest of the jacket!

Other problems? Well, you'll need to take care over nooks and crannies if you have more complicated figures than your rifleman – best done later with a fine brush – and to work at its best the airbrush needs to be kept scrupulously clean.

Aerosols My way of escaping the chores involved with cleaning an airbrush was to switch to aerosols, and although that was at the undercoat or primer stage, it is possible to use the same method when applying gloss paints. Some manufacturers of enamel paints designed for modellers do now sell them in aerosol containers, but you also will find that motor factors or supermarkets who stock aerosols intended for motorists offer a good selection of greens, reds, whites and greys.

The same technique should be used – alternately masking the top and bottom halves of each figure – and you will find that these paints dry very quickly.

In the previous section I mentioned that airbrushing eliminates the annoying problem of brush marks, and the same applies to aerosols. However, with both airbrushes and aerosols you must be careful not to leave an 'orange peel' finish – that slightly pimply look that results when the minute, individual particles of paint deposited on the figure being painted haven't joined together to form a glossy surface that is absolutely smooth. It can happen because the paint is too thick, or has been too sparingly applied.

'Runs' – paint that has run, then hardened into ridges (something like wax that has run down the side of a candle) – are usually associated with large flat surfaces, and on the small figures we are dealing with should rarely be cause for concern. Avoiding both runs and an 'orange peel' finish comes with experience; the technique of spray painting involves such factors as the consistency of the paint, the distance the spray nozzle is held from the surface being painted, and the shape of the spray pattern. Aerosols are pre-set, so you will be able to make adjustments only when using an airbrush.

Selecting and Mixing Colours I began this chapter by saying that toy soldiers are invariably finished using high gloss paints. I'm now going to qualify that statement: yes, all toy soldiers do have a high-gloss finish – but they are not necessarily painted with gloss paint.

If you pop into a good model shop you will find racks displaying a selection of paints that might include Humbrol, Tamiya, Gunze Sangyo, Humbrol Acrylic and Xtracolour. Modelling enamels such as Humbrol will be available in matt or gloss. There are also good, clear varnishes. Go into an art or craft shop and you can add to that list acrylics and oils by such well-known artist's suppliers as Rowney and Winsor & Newton.

Modelling of any kind is an individual pursuit in which the

modeller is answerable only to himself. The aim is perfection, and to get close to it – or at the very least achieve a satisfactory result – you will find yourself experimenting, and at times taking what might seem to be an unorthodox route. You will certainly do that in your sculpting, and painting also offers a number of interesting options.

When you use standard gloss paints you must, to a certain extent, be willing to compromise. No red will quite match British Scarlet; your Rifle Green will be acceptable, but not historically correct. You can get closer to a perfect match by mixing paints until your eye is satisfied – adding a touch of blue or yellow to the green to create the required hue – but this can be time-consuming, paints tend to change colour when they dry, and in any case judging colour is always a tricky business.

Flesh colour is available in a matt enamel, but a gloss flesh colour will have to be mixed. The basic colours to use are white, brown, yellow ochre and scarlet, but I have always achieved an excellent result by adding white to Humbrol Buff (No 7) to get the correct pallor, then bringing it to life with the merest touch of red.

After talking in rather general terms about the mixing and matching of gloss paints the question that immediately springs to mind is, Why haven't the manufacturers anticipated the problems faced by modellers seeking the correct colours for historical uniforms, and done something about it? The answer, of course, is that they have. Many years ago Humbrol introduced a limited range of authentic colours that include, for example, British Scarlet (MC1) and Polish Crimson (MC10) – but these, like their flesh (Matt 61), are matt enamels, and that's not quite what we want. Or is it?

If you are producing a range of toy soldiers for your own satisfaction and pleasure, there is no reason at all why you should not make full use of colours that will give authenticity without hard labour. Matt enamels are a pleasure to apply, they dry quickly, and one or two coats of clear varnish will enrich the hues so that they are a joy to behold. You will have your gloss finish and, in my opinion, the result can be superior to that achieved by using gloss paint.

I also mentioned acrylics. Used by a lot of military modellers, they can be applied straight from the bottle or tube, or thinned with water, and they are quick-drying. An acrylic finish has an attractive sheen, and if you use these colours on your toy soldiers you may well feel that a slight sheen is more attractive than full gloss. If not, then once again reach for the pot of varnish.

You are unlikely to use oil paints. Many military modellers do, and on individual miniature figures in all scales they achieve outstanding results. But oils take an age to dry, are rather expensive and using them on toy soldiers is, in my opinion, akin to decorating the inside of a garage with wallpaper costing £20 a roll.

However, I must again stress that, so far, you are in this for enjoyment (but see Chapter 9). The toy soldier purist who goes along to a retailer or an auction will be looking for soldiers to add to his collection, and he will want them painted with gloss enamels. But you are at the first stage of creating a unique collection; the figures are going to be created by you, and as you work you will have a grand vision of elegant cabinets displaying ranks of those figures.

How they are painted is entirely up to you.

Working to a System
Individual Figures

I have already mentioned that when modelling or painting it's a good idea to work from the skin outwards. The method was established in the constant search to find the easiest way of creating a sharp dividing line between two colours, or two pieces of equipment, and for most of the time it works well. However, like any rules, it is made to be broken, of which more later.

The principle is that if you paint a soldier's face and hands – a conventional skin-first start – you should do so without worrying about the dividing line between skin and uniform. Indeed, you should *deliberately go over that line*, thereby ensuring that every bit of skin is covered with flesh-coloured paint.

When the skin has dried, you paint the uniform – in this case the jacket. Soldiers of the 95th Rifles wore a green jacket with black collar and cuffs. These adjoin the skin of neck and wrists, so you will paint them next, now making a sharp dividing line where the collar and cuffs meet the skin, but going over the line where the collar and cuffs join the green uniform. Next you paint the jacket's main colour (rifle green), this time creating a neat line where the green meets the collar and cuffs, but painting over the edges of the waist and pouch belts that are worn over the jacket. Finally, you paint those belts black, ensuring that there is a neat dividing line between them and the green of the jacket.

I said that working outwards from the skin, layer by layer, works well most of the time, but of course there are occasions when you either find it impossible to stick to the rule, or feel more comfortable working in another way. Many modellers, for instance, will find it much easier to paint the cross belt before the jacket, then paint the green of the uniform up to the cross belt where there is a ridge for the brush to come up against rather than one for it to slip off. This is called *cutting back*, and you will find yourself doing it anyway if you make slips when using the flesh-first technique.

The important point about any system is that it should suit you. You may enjoy working in the reverse direction, starting with the top bits such as belts and merrily cutting back until you get to the skin, painting that last of all.

Now, before we move on to look at ways of painting a whole line of riflemen, a brief mention about the way you should hold the tiny soldiers while you are painting.

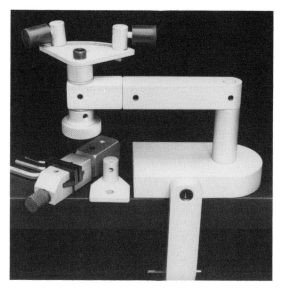

The Vice Squad, 'Main Unit' 2009. A device – which comes in various sizes – which enables a small model to be held securely and worked on at virtually any angle

Earlier in the book I talked about a Vice Squad device – ELS 2009 – which clamps to a bench or table, holds the miniature figure, and leaves both hands free. This is ideal for modelling or painting, and although it doesn't suit my style, I can heartily recommend it. But however good ELS 2009, or indeed any mechanical device, may be, I always find there is greater flexibility when a figure is held in the hand. I am right-handed, and my own method is to turn the palm of my left hand towards me, the hand drooping slightly, thumb on top, fingers below and slightly curled. The toy soldier fits neatly into the hand with the base resting on the tips of the curled fingers, the top of the hat resting under the ball of the thumb. The figure is easily rotated by moving the fingers – the hat swivels under the thumb's soft pad – and of course by turning your hand over so that its back is towards you, thumb down, fingers on top, you have turned the figure upside-down (and it can still be rotated).

Groups

On each individual within a group you will stick as closely as you can to one of the above painting systems, or one of your own with which you are comfortable. But when you have a lot of identical figures to paint – and particularly if you are a professional with a delivery deadline to meet – time becomes a factor, and you may well modify your chosen system to take account of paint drying times and other factors.

The easiest way to go about painting a number of figures is to

A close-up of a toy soldier being painted. The method of holding the figure is described in the text

tackle one colour, paint that bit of uniform or equipment on each figure, then go back to the beginning and start again with a fresh colour and a different part of the uniform. With the skin-first system, you would first paint all the hands and faces. If you are in a hurry, you might be disappointed to find that when you get back to the first figure, the flesh colour is still wet. Instead of waiting for it to dry, paint another colour that doesn't adjoin the hands or face; in the case of our rifleman, you could paint the green of the jacket and leave the black collar and cuffs to be painted next.

But, wait a minute! This time when you get back to the beginning of the line, the flesh is dry but now the green of the jacket is still tacky. So once again the black collar and cuffs must wait, and instead you paint all the grey trousers. Yes, that can be done – just – because the jacket and trousers are divided by the waist belt (there is a touch of green showing below the belt, so think ahead and when you paint the jacket, leave that scrap unpainted).

And so it goes on. Next time around you can, at last, tackle the collar, cuffs and pouch belt. You can't paint the boots or gaiters, because the trousers are still wet. If you are holding the soldier the way I suggested, the hat will be left until last because it rests under your thumb. What you can do is paint the hair and add some detail to the face: dots for the eyes, touches of red on the lips and cheeks.

As soon as you begin reading the above you will realize that the methods I suggest you use when painting a number of soldiers can also come in useful when painting a single figure. Indeed they can. One thing I will continue to stress about modelling toy soldiers is its sheer fascination, and when I told you that nothing can quite match the wonder of that first casting, I failed to mention that the sight of your first painted figure runs it a very close second. Impatience will spur you on, and rather than wait for bits of flesh to dry you will paint boots, belts, the topside of the base – anything, in fact, to avoid the inactivity that delays for one moment the time when your 95th Rifleman is finished, painted and ready for parade.

When painting a 54-mm figure, all bits are tricky. Well, not quite – although it may seem that way if you are painting in this scale for the first time.

General Painting Techniques

So far I've mentioned brushes and paints, but you will need to have at hand more paraphernalia than that to paint with confidence:

- paint
- knife or screwdriver (for prising off lids)
- brushes
- washing-up liquid
- thinners – a proprietary brand, or white spirit
- clean rags or tissues
- one or two clean jars
- a good, adjustable light
- a magnifying glass
- ventilation!

Brand new brushes can be brought to a fine point by moistening the tip between puckered lips (not recommended when you have washed them – the brushes, not your lips – in white spirit!).

Fine brushes – and that means all brushes when painting 54-mm figures – will have slim handles. If you have large hands, those slim handles can be made easier to hold by wrapping adhesive tape around them until you have achieved a comfortable thickness.

When painting broad areas such as jackets, trousers or flags and standards, load your brush with plenty of the required colour. For fine detail, you will use less paint, but always enough so that the brush runs freely without drag.

Never leave a brush loaded with paint. It is always best to have two jars of white spirit, so that you can wash the brush in one and rinse it quite clean in the other. Their fine points should always be restored after each rinse.

It's handy to have a rack for your paints, with a section for each colour. Ideal are the plastic boxes available from hardware stores. Most gloss enamels come in small tins. Prise off a lid only when you need a particular colour. When you have finished using it, wipe the lid and the inner rim of the tin before resealing. If you don't, a hard crust will form, and eventually you will be unable to close the tin. The usual advice is not to dip your brush into the tins, but to extract a small quantity of paint with a cocktail stick or something similar and place it on a makeshift palette. I must confess I find that method fiddly and time-consuming, and despite all that care the tins still get caked with dried paint.

Adjust your light so that it shines on the figure, and not in your eyes. Whether you are using one of the special holding devices I mentioned, or holding the soldier in your hand, your painting hand will need steadying. Your elbow will rest on the desk or table. The brush will normally be held between the tips of your thumb and index finger, and rest on your second finger. You do the necessary steadying of the whole hand with the little finger of the same hand, which rests wherever it can – against the base of the soldier, against part of your other hand, or on the holding device.

The rags you use should not leave fluff floating about in the air to settle where it will – usually on the nearest expanse of tacky paintwork. For the same reason, the room you work in and your immediate work surfaces should be kept reasonably dust-free.

Adding Essential Detail

Toy soldiers are simple souls, so tricky bits are only likely to occur if you strive for perfection. Look at any batch of old toy soldiers and you will see that the eyes are just black blobs – most of them quite close to where they should be. Paint will have been applied in the general vicinity of waist belts, dabs of gold paint will roughly indicate a buckle and the green of the base is likely to have strayed onto the boots. In some cases, paint will have been applied where nothing has been sculpted, which brings us back to the original question asked at the modelling stage: how much detail?

Some of you will have been quite content to create an extremely basic figure – jacket, trousers, boots and gaiters – either because you know that sculpting the finer detail is beyond you, or because you want to create a lot of toy soldiers as quickly as possible, in the image of those described above. If you have adopted that approach, then now is the time when all those details omitted at the modelling stage will be added with your paintbrush.

Pouch and waist belts are likely to be the largest bits of equipment left unmodelled, and you will paint these in using one stroke of, say, a Number 1 brush to establish a uniform width. Buckles can be added as blobs of brass or gold paint, and as you work your way down in size you will finish with three rows of tiny silver dots down the front of your rifleman's jacket – his buttons.

Such a figure subjected to careful, close-up scrutiny will look crude. Observed from a distance as an anonymous member of a group of identical figures, the effect will be charming and entirely compatible with the spirit of the true toy soldier.

But even at this stage that vexing question – How much detail? – is lurking in the background, and if you want to aim for perfection you will commit yourself to painting fine detail such as the snake buckle on your rifleman's belt, the light infantry buglehorn on the front of his hat or shako (rather than blobs of silver or gold), the precise details of the flintlock mechanism on the Baker rifle and the lettering on his water bottle that tells the world with which company and battalion of the 95th Rifles he serves.

Because each figure will be viewed as part of a group, it can be argued that painting any fine detail is a waste of time because it will never improve the overall effect. But that is looking at toy soldiers from the viewpoint of a casual observer. As the creator of the display you know each figure intimately, and what it boils down to is that the design that satisfies one modeller will be nowhere near good enough for another.

Advanced Painting Techniques

A little earlier I mentioned that instead of using gloss enamels you can paint toy soldiers with the matt variety, and create the gloss finish with a coat of clear varnish. If you have chosen that route you may well have considered adding some of the refinements so beloved of painters of connoisseur figures, so before moving on I'd like to give you a brief idea of what can be achieved, and how to go about it.

We see any figure as solid because of the effect of light and shade. If a military figurine, and that includes a toy soldier, is well sculpted and viewed in the right light, the shadows and highlights will be formed naturally. But painters of connoisseur figures have always enhanced those natural shadows and highlights by skilful paintwork, and there is no doubt that, when done artistically, the effect can be dramatic.

The technique is to create highlights with a lightened version of the basic matt colour, and create shadows with a darker shade. It works like this. Paint the face all over with the basic flesh colour. Now darken the flesh colour very slightly with a touch of black, and shade the eye sockets, under the nose, under the lower lip, and under the chin. If you wish you can also shade along the hairline, and beneath the cheekbones. Now add a touch of white to the basic flesh colour and use this to add highlights: a fine line along the top of the nose, a dab in the centre of the chin and on the cheekbones, and another short line just above each eyebrow.

The completed 95th Rifleman. When comparing this with the assembled casting you will notice that details such as buttons, belt buckle and shako (hat) badges have been added at the painting stage

These highlights and shadows must be blended in by tackling them before they dry with a brush moistened with white spirit. By gently stroking the moistened brush along the harsh dividing line between highlight or shadow and the main colour, it can be softened, creating a natural appearance.

Exactly the same technique is used to enhance the ridges and folds of jackets and trousers, and to make equipment stand out. The dark green paint used for your rifleman's uniform should be made even darker by adding a touch of black, then painted into folds, under waist and pouch belts and even, if you can manage it, under every button. Finally, paint along the top of each ridge or crease with a lightened version of the basic green, and blend in all shadows and highlights with your moistened brush.

The effect can be stunning, and when you have completed your soldiers by giving each one a coat of clear varnish, you will have a squad, battalion or regiment that will look realistic in even the poorest lighting: toy soldiers for the connoisseur.

8 Display

The world of military miniatures is inhabited by figures that can be diminutive 5-mm chaps that need to be viewed through a magnifying glass, or hefty fellows who are close to one-quarter life-size. Down at the bottom end of the range the mass of troops can form impressive displays such as the Waterloo diorama assembled by Captain William Siborne or they can be used for complicated wargames in which enthusiasts advance and retreat their forces across realistic battlegrounds.

Most military miniatures above 25 mm are collected for display. Connoisseur figures of 54 mm upwards are usually displayed individually, although small groups of two or three figures are popular. It is unusual for the larger figures to be part of a theme.

Because toy soldiers are always seen as large or small groups they offer unlimited scope for the most imaginative displays. As a maker of toy soldiers you will be more concerned with the figures themselves than the way they are packaged – indeed, you are unlikely to have packaging of any kind unless you decide to produce commercially – but because in some cases the boxes are important, I have made brief mention of them in this chapter on display. We will be discussing:

- display in boxes
- displaying to a theme
- suitable cabinets and lighting

An example of artistic paintwork on a mounted Royal Scots Grey. The figure was produced by Guards and Garrisons Ltd

- general care of toy soldiers
- gaining a modelling reputation
- creating sets to order
- a glance at the national and international scene

Display in Boxes   This can be a paradox, because the way some collectors treat their toy soldiers the only thing actually on display is the box! It might seem ridiculous for a toy soldier enthusiast to attend an auction, come away with a boxed set of early Britains and simply put it on the top shelf of the wardrobe, but that is certainly what happens. And, of course, the reason is that those collectors are buying with an eye to the future, and they know well that toy soldiers in their original box, itself in good condition, are going to be worth more than the same set unboxed.

A more sensible alternative for those who are fascinated by the figures themselves is to display the set of soldiers with the box lid removed. Although many modern makers use labels that simply present the firm's name, Britains designed a new label for each set they produced. Collectors might have, for example, boxes of 9th Queen's Royal Lancers, The 13th Hussars, 2nd

Dragoons, Montenegrin Infantry and Boer Infantry, and as well as having the name in suitably ornate writing the box lid would often be decorated with a stirring picture of the soldiers in action or on parade.

CBG Mignot (see Appendix A, p.131) catered for just this kind of display when they issued boxed showcases which featured such events as the meeting between Joan of Arc and the Dauphin; that one also included a detachment of knights facing halberdiers and crossbow-men.

Displaying to a Theme

I've already mentioned the impressive diorama of the Battle of Waterloo created by Captain William Siborne, and that and one of his later dioramas (1844) serve to illustrate two approaches to the intriguing prospect of creating a thematic display. The first took in an entire field of battle; the other focused on one particular skirmish at Waterloo, in this case the charge of the British heavy cavalry at the farm of La Haye Sainte.

Another example of a thematic display on the grand scale is described by Arthur Taylor in *Discovering Model Soldiers*, the charming little book that I mentioned earlier. In it Mr Taylor refers with some awe to a Major Harris, who undertook the monumental task of portraying the entire British Army as it was in the last years of full dress, from 1890 to 1914. Research, and drawing up what Major Harris called his Order of Battle, took two years. By the end of that time this eminent collector had completed plans for a force of 5,000 figures, comprising a Full Dress Corps, an Expeditionary Corps, a Naval Division and an Air Corps. Part of the breakdown of this immense force shows that cavalry regiments (three to each brigade) would be represented by three officers and twelve other ranks, and that each brigade would include a mounted band with bandmaster, kettledrummer and a dozen bandsmen.

That last paragraph neatly introduces you to another aspect of the toy soldier hobby that, for many, becomes at least as interesting as the actual modelling: historical research. You have already been involved in this in a small way when flicking through *Men at Arms* and other publications to discover the exact details of your toy soldier's uniform. But when you are planning a thematic display your concern will be not for the appearance of an individual soldier – you will go into that later – but with finding out details of the regiments involved in the battle or event that is your chosen theme.

For both Captain Siborne and Major Harris this was a labour of love that took several years to complete – and that was before the first soldier was placed in position; in Captain Siborne's case on a battlefield, in Major Harris' on a parade ground. Having read the above you are probably feeling somewhat dazed as you sit and contemplate your one, lonely 95th Rifleman. My suggestion is that when starting your own collection and visualizing how it will be organized and displayed you be reasonably ambitious without going overboard. In other words, rather than contemplating another reconstruction of the Battle of Waterloo, choose instead to represent those soldiers who took part in a relatively minor action. Then simply line them up in neat ranks in a display case rather than going to the additional labour of creating realistic terrain.

Out of History, into the Showcase

In 1802 the Experimental Corps of Riflemen was brought into the Line as the 95th (Rifle) Regiment. It arrived in Spain in 1808 and fought at Vimiera that same year (and continued to fight with Wellington in all the Peninsular battles until 1814). This battle would seem to be an excellent one with which to start displaying to a theme; you have, after all, got one miniature figure from the 95th!

For my research into this battle I turned to *The Peninsular War* by R.J. Wilkinson-Latham, a small paperback book in Shire Publications' 'Discovering Famous Battles' series (1973). Details of the British and Allied armies and the opposing French army include the total number of men involved on each side – being, respectively, 18,712 and 13,050. Quite a modest little battle; at Vittoria in 1813, four times that number participated on each side.

The British infantry consisted of eight brigades, each averaging three battalions. There were also 240 men of the 20th Light Dragoons, three batteries of artillery, and 2,000 Portuguese troops. Within the infantry brigades the Line battalions are listed by their numbers: the 1st Brigade comprised the 1/5th (the 1st battalion of the 5th Regiment), the 1/9th and the 1/38th, a total of 2,659 men.

The 2/95th were part of the 6th Brigade, while two companies of the 1/95th – of particular interest to us – fought with the 8th Brigade.

On the French side there were two divisions plus a reserve, a cavalry division and artillery numbering some 700 men.

All this gives you a lot of information about troops present on the field of battle, but doesn't tell you how to pack some 32,000 toy soldiers into a display case small enough to hang in your study. And, of course, you don't. Just as Major Harris did, you spend some time drawing up your own order of battle, and you do so based on a realistic assessment of the numbers you can display, and how soon you would like to complete the task.

I have said that the eight British brigades averaged three battalions. In fact there were eighteen full battalions and four, seven-and-a-half and two companies respectively of the 5/60th, the 2/20th and the 1/95th – a total of 21 Line regiments represented at Vimiera. So if you decided that the British infantry section of your display would consist of one officer and a private soldier from each of the numbered Line regiments present, you would have to produce a total of forty-two toy soldiers.

You can juggle that basic establishment as you choose. You might prefer to have an officer, sergeant, corporal and private soldier from each regiment, thus expanding your toy soldier requirement to eighty-four. Although that now seems to be a substantial number of figures it should be remembered that, as far as modelling is concerned, one example of each – officer, sergeant, corporal and private soldier – suitably painted, will serve to represent most of the regiments involved. For example, in the 1st Brigade the 1/5th (Northumberland) have gosling green facings on collar and cuffs, the 1/9th (East Norfolk) and the 1/38th (1st Staffordshire) both have yellow. Three identically modelled toy soldiers, with their facings painted in the appropriate colour, could march straight into the ranks of those three Line regiments, while other identical figures painted with white or black facings could join the 1/32nd (Cornwall) and the 1/50th (West Kent).

With one or two regiments, that approach won't work. If, for example, you decide to depict your highlanders – 1/71st (Highland Light Infantry) – in kilts, then you will need to model them separately, while officers of the 95th Rifles wore a fur-trimmed pelisse over an elaborately braided jacket, and for accuracy would certainly need to be individually modelled.

This business of collecting or displaying to a theme can be a fascinating business, for as well as becoming something of an expert on the uniforms worn by soldiers of days gone by you will also find yourself becoming engrossed in history. Most people will have heard of the Battle of Rorke's Drift (and Michael Caine), which took place during the first British invasion of Zululand in 1878. Some could tell you that the 2nd/24th (Warwickshire Regiment) – mainly Welshmen – were involved in the defence of the station. But I wonder how many would know that the three regiments of Zulus who stormed Rorke's Drift were the iNdluyengwe, the uThulwana and the uDloko, led by a Zulu *induna* named Dabulamanzi? If you decide to represent this famous battle – and have before you 'Men-at-Arms' No.57, *The Zulu War* – then you certainly will; and modelling the human form, out of uniform and resplendent in feathers from the ostrich, eagle's tail and widow bird, with a headband of leopard skin, neck ornamentation of cow tails and a kilt fashioned from the tails of many monkeys, will be a challenge that any serious modeller will relish.

Other wars and campaigns fought between colourful and disparate armies that make them ideal for thematic displays include the Crimean War (British/French/Turkish/Sardinians/Russians), The Jacobite Rebellions (Government Forces/Jacobites), The Sudan campaigns (Anglo-Egyptian/Dervish), The American Revolution (British/German Auxiliary/Loyalists/The Continental Army/The French Army/Indians), and the English Civil War. There are many, many more.

Suitable Cabinets and Lighting

While toy soldiers seen *en masse* are attractive in any situation – even lying battered and battle-worn in a cardboard box at a jumble sale – like most new collectors you will have grand ideas on the way you want your figures displayed. Because you are new to the game those grand ideas will be fairly hazy, yet it's pleasing to know that the choices lying before you are as many and varied as the historic campaigns whose haunting bugle calls will forever echo in the imagination.

Initially you will annex one shelf of a bookcase, standing on it your first solitary rifleman. Gradually he will welcome new recruits, postings-in – even re-enlistments and transfers from different regiments if you have begun converting existing figures. The group will begin to take shape, and as you rearrange the growing squad to its best advantage you will begin to have doubts about the lighting, realize that before too long you are going to need a second shelf and notice with chagrin the dust that has begun to settle on shiny paintwork.

When you inevitably decide that the time is ripe to move your growing collection into a dust-proof cabinet fitted with concealed lighting, you will be able to plan not only the way your collection is going to be displayed to its best advantage, but – if you are lucky enough to have a room for the purpose – the appearance and overall effect of the grouped cabinets you will eventually accumulate.

I know of one collector in Wales who keeps an eagle eye open for display cabinets being sold by local businesses that specialize in house clearances. He has bought several that are truly enormous; because he is buying second- or third-hand furniture his expensive collection is housed in dark wood cabinets built of solid oak that need to be placed in position by a crane. The overall effect is stunning. He is a collector, not a maker, so the toy soldiers he displays in these massive, glass-fronted cabinets are bought at auction and are themselves minor antiques; they complement each other, and the thoughtful placing of framed military prints under brass wall lamps, Wilton carpets that reveal dark polished floorboards, and a roll-top desk almost lost in the shadows where military books can be browsed through in comfort create, for this collector, not just a toy soldier display but his own private piece of history: the corner of an officers' mess, perhaps, at a remote hill station in India.

The same approach was adopted on a grander scale when the Forbes Museum of Military Miniatures was established in one wing of the Palais Mendoub in Tangier. Some rooms were unashamedly modern, with brightly lit display cases arranged along the walls in rows like aquaria. Others contained just one or two glass cabinets of great elegance, standing on vast expanses of tiled floor splashed by the Mediterranean sun that poured in through the arched windows of this splendid Moorish palace.

Mention of these outstanding collections will give you a good idea of what can be achieved, and as you read through those last paragraphs your mind was undoubtedly flitting ahead – wondering, perhaps, how you could get that Mediterranean sun to shine through the bare oak tree overhanging the garden shed. Short of moving the shed to Tangier, you can't; but what you can do is make a start, as that first collector did, by browsing around the second-hand shops for promising bits of furniture.

Old-fashioned china cabinets are ideal, often coming with double glass doors that are attractively curved. Deep bookshelves can often be found, and if you are a dab hand at carpentry you will find it easy to fit them with glass doors. Some kitchen wall units have glazed doors. The old stereo or hi-fi stack units that were popular in the 1970s have deep shelves and a hinged glass front.

While busy browsing you will have in your mind a picture of what your display will eventually look like, and if your inclinations lean more towards that richly furnished room in Wales than the palace in Tangier then the second-hand shops will be productive hunting grounds. However, if you are planning on something more modern, then you will need to turn to specialist manufacturers of display cases.

A typical advertisement in *Military Modelling* offers

'collectors' display cases created for miniature collections at miniature prices'. The cases are hand-made from softwood, mahogany-stained, and come with up to seven adjustable 6 mm glass shelves. The background can be a pleasing dark green or fawn. No mention is made of interior lighting, and because these cases are quite shallow – a maximum of about 50 mm – probably none is needed.

My own preference is for much deeper cases or cabinets that have their own interior illumination, and as well as having glass shelves I like them to be backed by a full-length mirror. This serves two purposes: it provides a rear view of every toy soldier and at the same time doubles the size of a toy army! The shallow cases described above are intended to display a single line of figures on each shelf, so the shelves can be set quite close to each other, allowing just enough clearance for the tallest of the miniature figures. The deeper cabinets I recommend will need to have their shelves set quite far apart; on each one you will have several ranks of toy soldiers, and in order to view the rear ranks there must be plenty of overhead space.

If this vision of massed ranks doesn't quite tally with my suggestion that your battle plan might include just four soldiers from each British regiment at Vimiera (officer, sergeant, corporal and private), remember that those four figures will make up one short rank, four figures from another regiment will be lined up behind them and so on to the back of the cabinet. And with different regimental uniform facings ranging from white through blue to black interspersed with such subtle shades as gosling green, bottle green, pea green, dark green, pale yellow, deep yellow, yellow and orange, you will see that such an arrangement – viewed under integral concealed lighting reflecting from the backing mirror and filtering through the glass shelves – can be a truly dazzling sight.

One final word before leaving display cases. A little earlier I remarked, tongue in cheek, that some of those once seen in the Palais Mendoub resemble aquaria. But for a small display that can be viewed from all sides, a modest aquarium is actually ideal – and if you are planning a centrepiece, most shops selling fishkeeping supplies offer aquaria with their own stands.

General Care of Toy Soldiers

Having made my final pronouncement on display cases, I will now return to them! And what I have to say concerns reports that are akin to a lot of advice dispensed nowadays: much of it is based on unproven research, and in any case doesn't necessarily apply to John or Joan Bloggs.

It has been suggested that, because of the properties of the wood, oak cabinets will have a detrimental effect on toy soldiers stored or displayed in them. Now that may well be, and if you want to play safe then by all means stick to cabinets made from supposedly safer timbers. But I believe that the research that unearthed this interesting fact was probably based on studies of old toy soldiers that had been stored in oak cabinets for many, many years. And while it may be accurate for those valuable old toy soldiers made from lead-rich alloys (which are in any case prone to 'lead disease' – a progressive deterioration of the metal usually caused by damp), for modern soldiers made from superior alloys which are richer in tin, bismuth and antimony, and protected by coats of modern gloss enamels, the same is not necessarily true; and in any case, just how many years go by before the effects become noticeable, and serious? As I say, the advice doesn't necessarily apply to, or concern, the ordinary modeller. My suggestion is that if you come across a beautiful oak display cabinet that is in good condition and unlikely to infest your house with woodworm, then buy it.

Apart from such serious and esoteric considerations as the effect of different timbers on alloys of lead, your main efforts at keeping your toy soldiers in pristine condition will be directed against dust, sunlight and unnecessary handling.

Even when they are kept in closed cabinets you will find dust collecting on your troops, and nothing yet invented can beat such a time-honoured weapon as the soft-haired paint brush. This will safely remove dust from the tiniest crevices, but because you will be picking up many of your soldiers, you must beware of fingerprints. If acid is the property of oak that causes damage, then the same applies to fingerprints, and just as an inspecting officer wears white gloves when carrying out a barrack room inspection, I would suggest you don a pair of light cotton gloves when dusting your troops.

Strong sunlight must be guarded against, but any householder who has watched curtains fade will know that already. You can avoid it by judicious positioning of your display cabinets, or by drawing the curtains on hot summer afternoons.

Naturally you will walk carefully between the cabinets as your establishment grows, knowing that a careless shoulder can produce a horrible noise like metal skittles falling. And if it is possible to lock your cabinets, then do so; you will be protecting your troops not against thieves, but against the curious.

Finally, as your collection grows in both size and value, do make sure that your troops are covered by your household contents insurance policy. With just one 95th Rifleman, standard cover should be sufficient; when you are looking at representatives of half the British and French armies, you will probably need to list them as high-risk items such as works of art.

Gaining a Modelling Reputation

Modelling toy soldiers is a funny business. On the one hand you get the slightly mocking raised-eyebrow treatment from people who hear what you do and obviously believe you have never grown up; on the other you have those same people staring open-mouthed when they eventually view your splendid, colourful display, and wondering, rather sheepishly, if you could possibly let them have a set.

This is the way you will gain a modelling reputation among friends and relatives, and how you treat their requests is entirely up to you. My own experience is that after some five years out of the business I have not a single set of my own soldiers (though I do have all the originals), while my brother-in-law has a set of 42nd Highlanders (the Black Watch) which he bought, and two mounted figures that were a Silver Wedding gift. One of my former painters has an impressive selection on a shelf. (I have recently taken up manufacturing again; this time I intend to keep one of every set I produce.)

Your fame can be spread far and wide if you decide to enter competitions that are held at various military modelling exhibitions. Perhaps the most famous of these in the UK is *Euro-Militaire*, an international military modelling exhibition which has been held in early autumn each year since 1986. Modelling standards are high, so it's no mean feat to walk away with a gold medal presented for the best model in a particular category, or even 'Best of Show'. And just in case I've fired your enthusiasm, among the purpose-built display cases I mentioned earlier there is a model with a soft fibre backboard on which awards can be pinned! It's actually designed for military badges, but what the heck …

Creating Sets to Order

Inevitably, as time goes by, an acquaintance who is impressed with your skills will express a yearning for a set of soldiers you have not yet produced. It might start off as a simple question: 'Why don't you make the Swiss Papal Guard?' Then when you state baldly that you're not particularly interested, that they don't fit into your order of battle, you will be told, 'but they're so unusual, so colourful — and you could probably sell quite a few sets …'.

Your acquaintance is hoping that thinly veiled references to potential profit will put ideas into your head and tip the balance in his favour; and indeed, once you start making sets to order you are dipping your toe, albeit tentatively, into the heady waters of commercial production. There is much more about that in the next chapter.

Money-making possibilities aside, I can think of one excellent reason for accepting a commission: you will be introducing freshness and light into the seemingly never-ending task of completing your order of battle. That may seem like heresy, yet staleness can reveal its insidious effect in deteriorating quality. You want your Vimiera display to be of the highest standard, and the sheer joy of modelling figures that have been suggested to you out of the blue will stimulate your creative juices and pay dividends when you return to your order of battle. There is a bonus, besides: you will always have the moulds for that 'one-off' set, and there are plenty of shelves to fill in those roomy display cabinets you picked up at the local auction ...

Another figure by Guards and Garrisons Ltd. Some paint has chipped off the rifle sling, but the fine detail on the mitre cap can clearly be seen

A Glance at the National and International Scene

I've already mentioned the possibility of your displaying your rapidly improving modelling skills at exhibitions, but to people on the fringes of the military modelling hobby that may seem like a case of 'easier said than done'. This, surely, is a minor recreation. There can't be that many people who spend their leisure hours making toy soldiers, so where and when are these exhibitions held?

At the time of writing (1995), the notice-board pages in the two issues of *Military Modelling* I have before me give a fair indication of the continuing, worldwide popularity of the hobby. It also suggests that if you do want to display your talents on a larger stage, you won't need to travel all that far from home.

Welling Model Club was holding its open day at the town's

community centre in April, the Wirral Modelling Club was holding its third annual show in the Centenary Stand function rooms at Liverpool Football Club in May. On a larger scale, the East Midland's Model Show was to be held at the Hinckley Leisure Centre in March, the North East Modelling Society was holding a two-day modelling exhibition at the Borough Hall, Hartlepool, in July, the Northern Model Show was to be held at the Temple Park Centre, South Shields, in June, and the Woodvale International Rally was taking place – at RAF Woodvale, near Southport – in August, and would include militaria.

Of particular interest to readers of this book is the fair staged by Charles Davis and Richard Windrow. Their International Toy Soldier Fair is now in its fourth year, and the venue in March 1995 was the Banqueting Suite of the Metropole, The Leas, Folkestone.

Two other international events were advertised: the Danish Military Historical Society 50-year jubilee exhibition ran from October 1994 to February 1995 at the Royal Danish Armoury Museum, Copenhagen, and the Southeastern Toy Soldier Show, sponsored by the South Carolina Military Miniature Society, was to be held in August, the chosen venue being the South Carolina State Museum, Columbia, South Carolina, USA.

Another regular show is held by the Aldershot Branch of the British Model Soldier Society, and I make particular reference to this one because the prestigious British society of which it is a branch held its Diamond Jubilee celebrations throughout 1995. Events were held in Ealing and Wandsworth in London, and in Poole, Salisbury and Plymouth.

9 The Toy Soldier Business

By modelling a one-off set of toy soldiers for a friend you will have taken your first step along the road leading to full-scale commercial production. Whether you take the second and subsequent steps depends on your own inclinations and aspirations, and these will be influenced by factors that include the success or otherwise of your current vocation. Even if you are weary of your present job and feel like a change, modelling toy soldiers as a commercial proposition is not necessarily the answer; it can be said of most hobbies that what is a pleasurable pastime when conducted part-time can become hard labour when converted to a business.

If you feel that there is money to be made from a hobby which gives you great pleasure, then perhaps the answer is to begin limited production as an adjunct to your main occupation. This gives you the best of both worlds: your main income will remain secure, while you will have the considerable pleasure of seeing your own toy soldiers talked about and written about, and bask in the knowledge that they are displayed on the shelves of collectors all over the world.

Whichever route you choose, you will need to know about:

- assessing the market place
- creating a business image

The littered work bench of a professional pattern maker

- centrifugal casting systems
- outworkers
- working methodically
- advertising
- final thoughts

Assessing the Marketplace

If you go out into the streets of your home town, armed with a clipboard, and conduct your own market survey, you will probably find that after a tiring day your sheet of paper is still blank; somehow, the hordes of toy soldier collectors you were expecting to meet have passed you by. This sounds depressing. If you were contemplating selling lawn mowers and got the same result, you would immediately drop the idea. Toy soldier collectors are out there, but you need to reach them – that is, market your own soldiers – in an unconventional way.

Back in the 1980s I took my first tentative step into commercial production by making 75-mm military miniatures that were passable but certainly didn't take the collecting world by storm. I persevered for a while, then took a shrewd look at the market, sat down with a block of Plasticine and modelled one toy soldier. A silicone rubber mould followed, and a day or so later I had cast and painted six toy soldiers.

My next step was to send that set to *Military Modelling* magazine. At that time they had a column called 'Atten-shun', which reviewed all new products. It still exists, but now it deals with connoisseur figures and there is a second monthly column called 'Soldier Box' that reviews the many toy soldiers that are regularly released.

This is the wide window into which collectors and dealers look each month. And because *Military Modelling* is the 'world's best-selling military modelling magazine', your set of toy soldiers will be gazed upon by military modelling *aficionados* all over the world – but in particular in the United States.

I was completely unprepared for what followed. The magazine took a little time to write and publish their review of my toy soldiers (which extolled their excellence), and while that was happening I took a second sample set to *Under Two Flags*, a well-known military miniature shop in Wigmore Street, London. They were bought by the owner, Jock Coutts (who also ordered a further eight sets), and I was delighted to receive a telephone call from him the next day informing me that the first set had been snapped up by a collector not long after I left the shop. This is the heady stuff that makes everything worthwhile.

Within a short time *Military Modelling* went on sale, and plopped through the letterboxes of subscribing collectors and dealers overseas. And during the next few weeks I got three phone calls from the United States: one from Cowin Enterprises of New York, a second from Dutkins of Philadelphia, and the third from Mickey's House of Soldiers in California. All placed large orders. Later I heard from collectors in Canada, Australia, South Africa and Italy. Those toy soldiers that began life as a shapeless block of Plasticine were suddenly in demand; Union Jacks were on their way.

And when that happens to you, you must be prepared.

Creating a Business Image
What's in a Name?

Britains toy soldiers had a ready-made name that inspired patriotism and told collectors all over the world where these original hollow-cast figures originated. You will have to dig deep to come up with a business name that has the same effect, pleases you and tells potential customers what you are selling. The latter isn't terribly important, because you will be advertising in publications that are dedicated to military miniatures.

I mentioned Britains, and although their name was almost too good to be true, a further descriptive tag was needed on the bright red box to entice collectors (or young boys, because Britains were established when toy soldiers really were toys). Usually this was the name of the regiment: Montenegrin Infantry, the 13th Hussars and so on.

"UNION JACKS"

An example of a set of toy soldiers, lined up in front of their labelled box

Some modern manufacturers choose this approach, using a single name with a descriptive tag: Trophy Miniatures (Wales), Dorset Soldiers (England), Regal Collector Figures (New Zealand). Others are much more colourful and imaginative: Great Britain and the Empire and Boys of the Old Brigade are just two examples.

I began in a conventional way by incorporating my own name: Paxton Sheriff Miniatures. Three years later I formed a limited company. It would have been quite acceptable to simply tack the 'Limited' onto the end of the original name, but I recalled that back in the mid seventeenth century when, after the Restoration, 'army' was a hated term, the troops that looked after the personal safety of Charles II and secured the kingdom against its enemies were known as 'Our Guards and Garrisons'. This seemed to me to be a splendid name and accordingly I formed Guards and Garrisons Ltd.

Much later, when I returned to commercial production in 1995, I chose to call my business Magna Carta, and I've no doubt that you will find considerable enjoyment, and some enlightenment, as you search the history books for an eye-catching name.

Boxes and Labels   Most toy soldiers are presented in red boxes. This is not an inviolable rule. There is nothing wrong with using handsome royal blue boxes, or others of a pleasing green. One possible approach is to adopt different colours for different arms of the services, or different branches of the same arm – foot soldiers, cavalry, artillery.

Your boxes will need to be deep enough to take soldiers lying flat on their backs, and although this seems to indicate a requirement for shallowness, remember that figures in certain poses can create problems: soldiers standing at ease will have fragile rifles or muskets thrust forwards; rifles carried at the slope will create front and rear projections. So, do you order one standard box size to take everything up to the most awkward pose you can imagine, or do you have your boxes tailor-made for each set produced? My suggestion is that if you intend to sell most of your soldiers in sets of six, then boxes of a standard size are your best bet. At a push, awkwardly posed figures can be packed on their sides. And if you make the occasional massed band, then at that time special flat, square boxes can be bought.

This same dilemma will confront you when you are designing a label. When running Guards and Garrisons Ltd I produced sets of British soldiers from the Jacobite Rebellions, the Seven Years War, the American Revolution, the Napoleonic Wars and the Zulu Wars. These were all marketed under the label 'Union Jacks'. English Civil War figures bore the label 'Kinsmen', while their counterparts in the American Civil War were labelled 'Old Glory'.

Although I produced many different soldiers from a number of campaigns (1751 Grenadiers, for example, could be painted to represent any one of approximately 100 regiments of foot), I never needed more than those three labels. Distinctive labels for each set are an attractive proposition, but you will need to balance the desire for attractive and individual presentation with the cost of designing and printing many different labels.

One quick reference to modern technology. Although most labels are designed and printed by commercial firms and thus come with 'crack backs' (adhesive protected by a peelable film), desk-top publishing programs mean that if you invest in a computer and colour printer you can produce your own with minimum effort. Many labels completely cover the box lid (mine always did), but some are much smaller and my own feeling is that a small label that leaves the lid's own rich colour exposed is an attractive alternative.

Before we leave boxes and labels we must tackle the problem of how to secure the individual soldiers in their container. Years ago the figures were sewn in, or retained with small loops of elastic (I believe Britains still use this method for special sets).

From the beginning I always wrapped each figure in the type of acid-free tissue paper used for protecting jewellery, placing a few layers in the box and lid and making sure that each figure was swathed in enough to ensure they were tightly packed.

I later discovered that Dutkin's of Philadelphia used to unwrap each of my soldiers, and fit each box with foam inserts into which six slots had been cut. One soldier fitted into each aperture, a method that has the advantages of being labour-saving, totally secure (the box and lid were also lined with foam), and of allowing the soldiers to be viewed when the lid is removed.

A Unique Product When setting out in business you will need to look at the toy soldiers currently on sale, and decide on your own approach.

Some manufacturers adhere rigidly to the traditional look, making toy soldiers that are intentionally crude – uncomplicated sculpting, basic painting techniques. Others have opted for realism, creating fine detail in both the modelling and painting, producing sets of soldiers that are virtually six gloss-painted connoisseur figures. In between there are a host of manufacturers who, either from deliberate policy or limited design skills, produce soldiers which are neither crude nor exquisite, but nevertheless fulfil that criterion which I have emphasized is the inherent charm of the toy soldier: they look attractive *en masse*.

Although you will have established your own style long before you contemplate commercial production, you may need to adjust it to meet the demands of your chosen niche in the marketplace. The cruder toy soldiers are easily mass-produced. More detailed figures – and here I refer particularly to the painting, which must be done by hand on each soldier – are difficult to produce in quantity without allowing standards to suffer. So you must know exactly what you are setting out to achieve. Do you want to sell vast numbers of soldiers at low profit margins, or smaller numbers of exclusive toy soldiers bearing a high mark-up?

In one respect only, your decision is of no consequence. For whichever route you choose, you will certainly need to investigate the various methods of automated casting in order to keep up with the demands of impatient customers.

Centrifugal Casting Systems The simplest of centrifugal casting systems is the mould box and counterweight mounted on a primitive turntable which is spun by hand. Its main drawback is that although detail on the casting is always crisp, only one figure can be produced at a time. Nevertheless it is possible by this method to produce perhaps twenty figures an hour if all is going well. Four hours' casting and you will have eighty figures lined up, enough for more than a dozen boxes of six soldiers. In the early days of your business that will be sufficient to keep you busy for a full week, and provide a reasonable income.

No doubt some brainstorming and ingenuity would improve the system. You could add a second mould box instead of the counterweight I mentioned earlier, and if some way of feeding metal from a central point to both boxes could be rigged then production would be doubled (in theory: in practice you would waste time fiddling with two boxes, thus reducing the gains). But now we are reaching that dangerous point where all your efforts are being expended in devising crude casting systems instead of getting on with the job of design and production, and the sensible option is to look at professional machines. You will also save wear and tear on your back.

Centricast

Not too long ago, switching from hand pouring to a centrifugal casting system meant everything changed: you worked with unfamiliar machines and used different materials. Some change is unavoidable, but the system devised and marketed by Alec Tiranti Ltd is reasonably priced, compact, and allows you to continue working with the now familiar silicone rubber.

The basic principle of centrifugal casting is very simple. At higher speeds than I could manage using my converted swivel chair the castings produced are beautiful to behold, and with all centrifugal casting systems it is possible to produce a number of figures from a single pouring.

It goes like this. A central turntable is driven by an electric motor. On that turntable a circular mould is mounted. The mould, like a Victoria sandwich cake, consists of a top and bottom slice – equivalent to the two halves of your first two-piece mould. The impressions of the half-dozen or so soldiers you are about to cast are inside the sandwich and radiate from its centre like the spokes of a wheel. At the mould's centre there is a pouring hole. The machine is set in motion, the circular disc spins and the correct quantity of molten metal is poured into the central hole. After a few seconds the machine is stopped, the mould is taken from the turntable and when the sandwich is opened it is found to be filled with six perfect castings.

There is more to it than that, of course. But instead of casting eighty figures in an exhausting four hours you will have the capability to produce, with comparative ease, six times that

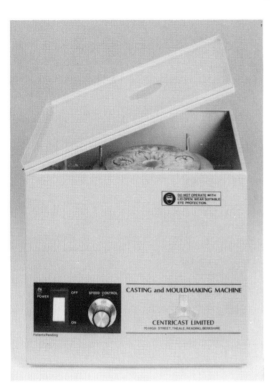

The Centricast System, a compact machine which utilizes centrifugal force to make moulds and cast objects and figures

number in the same time. Eighty boxes of soldiers. You will be able to build up a stock of unpainted castings, so that when those big orders come you are well prepared to meet pressing delivery dates.

The complete Centricast system comes in a package containing everything you need to commence production (except a thermostatically controlled melting pot). The essential difference between this system and all others is in the mould-making process.

Vulcanized Moulds

You have become familiar with the cold-cure silicone rubbers that you have used to make strong, re-usable moulds. Equipment has been minimal: mixing bowls and stirrers, the silicone rubber and catalyst, simple mould boxes. When making your moulds no heat or pressure has been involved, and the beauty of these rubbers – when used in moulds suitable for hand pouring or in a Centricast system – is that because shrinkage in the mould-making process is negligible the castings produced from such moulds are virtually the same size as the original master figure.

Another distinct advantage when making moulds from silicone rubber is that you can use delicate master figures; for a one-piece mould, wax or Plasticine are both suitable.

Traditional centrifugal casting systems use much bulkier equipment. The principle is always the same – circular sandwich moulds with impressions radiating from a central pouring hole, spun on a turntable – but the moulds themselves are of heavy black rubber. To make them you must have a bulky vulcanizing press (500 lbs) which uses heat and pressure; from master to finished castings there is shrinkage, there can be some distortion, and the master figures you use must be able to withstand great heat and pressure. The advantage is that the moulds are very strong, and it is likely that you can produce more figures during the life of a mould than you can when using silicone rubber.

Briefly in this system the two halves of raw black rubber are pre-warmed on the electrically heated plates of the vulcanizing press. They are then removed to the workbench where the bottom half is placed in a vulcanizing frame consisting of a steel hoop perhaps 40 mm deep – of the same diameter as the rubber mould – and circular steel plates to seal top and bottom (when closed it looks like a flat, circular steel box up to 280 mm in diameter). The master figures are positioned inside the vulcanizing frame on the smooth rubber surface of the bottom half of the rubber sandwich, together with locating studs and a sprue former (to create the central pouring hole). The top half of the sandwich is then placed in position. Because the mould – packed with master figures – is now deeper than the mould ring, the top half stands proud, preventing the top steel plate from seating. The vulcanizing frame is carefully transferred to the vulcanizing press, where a pressure of several tons is applied by means of an integral jack. This forces the top plate down onto the mould ring, compressing the pre-heated rubber inside the vulcanizing frame, and into the fine detail of each master figure. With the vulcanizing frame effectively sealed and under pressure, a temperature and time is set, and the mould is left to vulcanize, or cure.

Outworkers

The sight of eighty boxes of gleaming metal toy soldiers lined up on your shelves – almost 500 individual miniatures – is so impressive to a toy soldier fanatic that as you step back to admire the array the fact that each figure must be hand painted seems but a minor irritation. But when realization sinks in (usually when the first big order arrives on your desk) a hasty calculation tells you that the task can never be completed by one person in the time available.

My own method, an almost universal practice, was to employ outworkers to 'bulk paint'. Working quickly, they would splash on the scarlet jackets and grey trousers, the flesh colour on hands and face, the black of boots and helmets, the green of bases. They were instructed to do this to the best of their ability, ensuring that each coat of paint applied was rich and glossy, but worrying rather less about dividing lines. Outworkers were chosen with care, and many were, or became, skilful painters. Several boxes of soldiers were delivered to each outworker at the beginning of a week and collected when ready. And once the bulk-painted soldiers were back in my workshop, I was able to sit down with my brushes and pots of paint, tidy up the overall paint job, and apply the finishing touches.

You can advertise for outworkers in a number of ways: through newspaper advertisements, the local Job Centre, or by word of mouth. But the only certain way of selecting suitable painters from those that apply is to give them a trial set of soldiers to paint.

Outworkers take the job surprisingly seriously, and you will find their antics laughable, tragic, and downright infuriating. One young man I employed lived on a farm. In order to dry the soldiers he was painting he lined them up on the fender in front of an open coal fire – and a fall of soot left each Napoleonic Grenadier looking like a Victorian chimney sweep. Another family group – definitely union-influenced – decided that the wages I was paying weren't enough, convened a meeting in their kitchen to which I was invited and told me bluntly that if there was no more money on the table they must, reluctantly, withdraw their services.

You will, of course, need to keep records of all outworkers employed, and the wages paid. It's unlikely that any will earn enough money to become liable for Income Tax or National Insurance, but you may still need to make annual returns to the Inland Revenue.

Working Methodically   If your toy soldier business is run part-time for pocket money, when a set or two sell you can nip out and buy yourself that revolutionary new putter or a gleaming metal wood; when they don't you can put your moulds away and spend a few evenings playing cricket with the kids.

If, however, the business is run to pay the mortgage and to buy the month's groceries, you'll need to do some planning. Your aims must be to design the right soldiers at the right time, to mass-produce them with speed and efficiency, to be fanatical about quality control, and to ensure that the glistening figures don't gather dust on your shelves. Unsold stock is always dead money.

You can rarely make a living by relying on orders from private collectors. Dealers and model shops all over the world must be made aware of your products, and it's the big orders from them that will give your business a degree of stability. I say that with some reservations because orders will always run hot and cold, and once you start selling overseas you will also be subject to fluctuating exchange rates. My business did extremely well in the mid 1980s when the dollar and pound were almost at parity, not so well when the pound was particularly strong.

Designing   It's a big step from the early days when you are marketing one box of toy soldiers to the time when you are able to present a catalogue listing dozens of different sets. Whether it is a lucrative, or even an economically viable, step can depend on the thought that you put into your design work. And, of course, by that I don't mean the skill that goes into the conception of each soldier, but in the way you produce sets based on your own assessment of the marketplace.

I've already mentioned how you can choose between the cruder, traditional toy soldiers and the modern trend towards more detailed figures. But you must also try to establish what is currently popular with today's collectors, or attempt to produce soldiers from an era or a war that hasn't been done before – not because it's unpopular, but simply because nobody has made the effort.

My own steps into commercial production were taken blind: I liked the look of eighteenth-century British Grenadiers with their mitre caps, and modelled one without thinking of painting difficulties. In fact each mitre cap has the white horse of Hanover on the small front flap, the Royal crest or a regimental design on the main body of the cap, and other bits and bobs on the reverse – all on a hat perhaps 7 mm high! Production went ahead, and it transpired that by sheer accident I had hit on a range of attractive figures that no other toy soldier manufacturer was producing, and because I had no prior knowledge of toy soldiers the sculpting and painting were of standards previously not attempted. However, because I was determined that every detail of those mitre caps would be faithfully reproduced, I was always involved in lengthy painting sessions when the bulk-painted figures returned from the outworkers. The result was that the volume of Union Jacks produced was decided by how fast I could paint.

Of course, since then many manufacturers have matched that high quality; but my ruminating in this way is intended to set you thinking about the way you are going to take the toy soldier world by storm.

Production

At its simplest, you don overalls and begin a morning's haphazard casting at the end of which you have x number of figures representing a variety of different regiments.

Later that day the second post arrives bringing an order from one of your US distributors. He wants twenty sets of Imperial Chinese Infantry from the Boxer Rebellions – and because they have deep undercuts and are always tricky to extract from the moulds, those are the sets you didn't cast!

So how *do* you plan your casting sessions. Do you periodically work through your catalogue, casting one or two sets from every one listed? Do you cast only those sets you know are selling well? Or do you refuse to cast anything for stock, preferring instead to cast to order?

I must confess that my own inclination was always to cast to order. With modern equipment the process is quick and easy, and if an order comes in with the morning mail, by lunchtime you can have the required sets ready for your outworkers to begin painting. True, if the figures are already on your shelves they can be delivered to the bulk-painters by coffee break; but if you do keep a stock, the sets on the shelves don't happen to match the order and you're also running short of tin alloy, you can find yourself tossing perfectly good soldiers back into the melting pot.

Another aspect of production that must be mentioned here, particularly if you decide to cast to order, is the maintenance of your moulds. All rubber moulds suffer wear and tear. A tiny section torn away means a corresponding raised lump of metal on the figure, yet the natural tendency is to keep using those worn moulds and put up with the nuisance of extra cutting and filing. When time is of no consequence, little harm is done, but you will find yourself working flat out unnecessarily if a large order comes in and you are using excessively damaged moulds. Put up with minor damage, by all means. But when it's obvious that you are making work for yourself and hindering smooth production, make a new mould.

Painting   Painting needs to be planned in two ways. First, at the design stage you must decide on the standard you are going to set for the finished toy soldiers (and that is ultimately going to be down to your skill). And secondly, you must consider the logistics involved in dealing with outworkers.

The first appears to be easy, but in fact will in part be determined by the skill of your outworkers, and at the outset you haven't got any. So whatever standard you set you are inevitably going to do a great deal of painting while your business becomes established, much less if you are fortunate enough to employ good, reliable painters. If you have designed simple figures with reasonably plain uniforms – they do exist, as you know, and can be surprisingly impressive – your own involvement at this final stage will be kept to a minimum.

Outworkers have already been discussed, and apart from the problems already mentioned your main concerns, once you have recruited your team of suitable painters, will be with keeping them supplied with materials such as paint, brushes and white spirit, and with the delivery and collection of toy soldiers.

Supply of materials is straightforward. For transporting the raw castings and finished figures you will need suitable boxes (with greater protection afforded for the freshly painted soldiers on the return journey). Your transport costs will be higher if you live in a rural area – as I do – for your painters are likely to live many miles apart.

The speed your outworkers can achieve will only be established over a period of time. Once you know each person's work rate you will be able to set deadlines when you deliver. Inevitably there will be wide variations in both quality and speed, and you will have some painters who can be relied on to do quick work in an emergency, others whose work is first class, but cannot be hurried.

Finally, it's often possible to leave some of the assembly work to outworkers. One of my own painters once worked for a firm called Steadfast (still going strong), and told me how castings from them arrived by post in bits and pieces and needed to be glued together before he could begin painting. If you have people with the necessary skills, by all means make use of them. You will certainly need to pay them extra.

Distributing

I once worked through the night to get several sets of figures painted; my son delivered them to north-east England the next day, very gingerly, for some were still tacky. In the early days of my business, fragile cardboard boxes which were much too large were packed with toy soldiers and sent by air to the United States. They arrived, albeit with some internal damage. Boxes of considerable strength made the same trip, and arrived empty, and in tatters. Others disappeared without trace.

You will find yourself making countless trips to the Post Office to send consignments ranging from a single box of toy soldiers to one of fifty or more (and to claim compensation for consignments lost). You will make use of first-class mail, parcel post, and air freight, and you will be involved with customs declarations and bills of lading; even, as I once was, with the United States Embassy whose officials were the only people able to give me a direct answer to the question, 'Must the country of origin be clearly marked on the base of each individual figure?' (In the case of small toy soldiers the answer, I believe, was 'no'.)

Inland distribution causes no problems (other than that of cost), while the technicalities involved in the export of your toy soldiers are outside the scope of this book. Government departments such as that of Trade and Industry provide mountains of bumf. As well as detailing export regulations, they also list wholesalers and retailers in almost any country you care to name, with details of the goods they require.

Advertising Some pages back I mentioned that market research on the streets of your home town would lead to the impression that selling toy soldiers is like flogging a dead horse. Following on from that, it's clear that advertising your toy soldiers in general publications is going to get you nowhere (one possible exception being Exchange & Mart, which is the UK's premier paperback marketplace for anything and everything).

Just as enthusiastic philatelists have their own magazines, so toy soldier collectors have magazines that are either devoted to the subject or include some toy soldier columns, new product reviews and classified advertisement sections. These are the publications you will go to when you wish to advertise your wares, and as with most kinds of advertising your choice will lie between the simple classified columns that are priced on lineage or the number of words, and larger display advertisements that take up a full page, half page, and so on, and can include colour or black-and-white photographs.

Any advertising, whether it's a one-off or a planned campaign, costs money. But there are other ways of getting your glistening toy soldiers before the eyes of the buying public, and one of the best is by sending sets you produce to be reviewed by a magazine. I have already described the results when I sent my sets to *Military Modelling*, and the only rider I would add to that is that you must be prepared to accept some criticism. No review is of any use if it praises unreservedly every new product it receives, and one benefit to be gained from this kind of 'free' advertising is that your models are being looked at by experienced eyes. If there are faults, then you need to know about them – and sometimes close study of photographs of your soldiers will enable you to spot anatomical or design faults that have gone unnoticed.

Incidentally, in the preceding paragraph I deliberately put 'free' in quotation marks because there is one price you pay for your review: the reviewer invariably keeps the set of soldiers!

As time goes by you will have a growing list of customers who have bought from you. I found that toy soldier collectors are mostly friendly and talkative people, and if they like what you supply they will always let you know. Not only is this praise welcome, but the goodwill it demonstrates should be put to good use. A mailshot to all your customers is always worthwhile when you bring new sets out, but you might like to extend this service into a regular newsletter, perhaps incorporating an order form. If you plan your production you can, in this way, get advance orders for soldiers still on the drawing board. And as your newsletters are likely to be retained, and passed around, they can generate orders that seem to arrive out of the blue.

Final Thoughts

In arriving at the prices you will charge for your boxed sets, you will have taken into account the various costs incurred during the production process: everything from the pencils used to sketch an original design right through to final postage costs. You may need professional help with this; accountants have the expertise, and nowadays the major banks offer excellent packages for new businesses that include printed sheets on which to work out your business plan, and start-up costs. In your quest for sales you will explore all avenues, and it's worth remembering that not all toy soldier collectors want to buy complete sets. A box of soldiers that sells for anything up to £50 can be split into individual painted toy soldiers selling for £8 each, and your overall profit can be greater as you will save on both boxes and labels (an individual soldier can be wrapped in tissue and posted in a Jiffy bag).

Unpainted castings are also popular. Many collectors enjoy painting and assembling, and £3 for an unpainted casting pleases them and again reduces your own workload. Such items can be packed individually, unassembled, in the type of self-sealing transparent plastic envelopes available from commercial stationers, then popped into a Jiffy bag for posting.

Finally, there is one other service you can offer to potential customers, and this is the making of sets to order. You are likely to get commission enquiries from collectors seeking a particular set that they have been unable to find on any manufacturer's lists, and others who simply want something unique.

Naturally, you will have to think long and hard over your fees. One point to consider is that you are committing a lot of your time to the design and manufacture of a set that is going to sell just the once. It's not much use plucking figures out of the air, but if you calculate on selling 100 of each of your boxed sets, over a period of time, then the income from each is going to be well over £4,000. Although collectors seeking a unique set expect to pay well for it, you certainly cannot charge that amount. But against the potential profit from a set that will sell over and over again you will have to weigh the immediate gain of perhaps a tenth of that – say, £400. It will certainly help your cash-flow, and your satisfied customer is likely to return. You may also get regular orders for one-off sets from people who intend starting a toy soldier business, but have no sculpting or painting skills.

Your lists, therefore, should comprise three sections (but see next chapter): boxed sets, individual painted soldiers and unpainted castings. Tack a little note on the end announcing your willingness to accept commissions, and as far as the world of toy soldiers goes you have created a business that offers all things to all men but in particular, I would suggest, a great deal of satisfaction to you.

10   Digressions

One of the joys of having a number of castings of different soldiers available is that it is rarely necessary to begin modelling any new soldier from the armature, or even the Minikin, stage. It's easier, and often quicker, to modify an existing, well-proportioned figure than it is to begin all over again the process of measuring in fractions of millimetres. Many hobbyists working on larger figures do this all the time. It's known as converting, and as far as I can recall every single figure after my original 1751 Grenadier was a conversion (no, there was one exception: an American Civil War cavalryman, seated cross-legged, for which I had no equivalent).

Although a metal casting is rigid, judicious cutting and filing can make it easy to adjust even the most complicated poses. Sometimes you will cut off a figure's head so that it can be replaced at a different angle, and cut completely through the torso at the waist so that the upper portion can be turned slightly to left or right.

More often your conversion will entail nothing more than the repositioning of arms and legs, and to do this without distortion you must look at human joints and see how they move. The knee and elbow are both simple hinges that move in one direction only, and to bend or straighten them on your miniature figures you should cut a deep vee behind the hinge: that is, in the hollow behind knee or elbow. Once the position of the limb has been adjusted, the cut section can be filled in with Milliput in the usual way.

Converting

122

Shoulders are more complicated. To raise an arm so that it is outstretched you will need also to study the way the shoulder lifts, and in these cases it is usually best to do major surgery: cut the arm off, reposition it, and use Milliput to adjust the look of the shoulder.

A figure that was standing square but is being converted to one standing with all the weight on one leg will need to have the other leg fractionally bent, the horizontal line through the hips tilted one way and that through the shoulders tilted the other. The vertical centre line will have moved from a central position to one side as the weight has shifted over the braced leg, and the figure will need to be studied carefully so that a balanced pose is maintained.

Once the body and limbs are in the new position, conversion of the uniform is straightforward basic modelling. Unwanted garments or equipment will be cut or filed away and the replacements built up with Milliput.

A natural result of the surgery done when converting is that you will build up a box of spares. There will be heads, arms, legs, a variety of torsos and sundry bits of equipment such as packs, pouches, blanket rolls, water bottles, powder flasks and haversacks. All of this simplifies your work, for if you begin modelling a soldier from the Seven Years War, for example, you will probably have most of the equipment you need, ready made, in your spares box.

Civilian Figures
Many toy soldier companies also produce excellent ranges of civilian figures in exactly the same scale. My own were produced exclusively for an American distributor, and once I embarked on them there was an immediate feeling of freedom.

Every detail of a toy soldier's uniform must be faithful to the real life original; if you put the wrong number of button loops on a grenadier's jacket the error will certainly be noticed by collectors who have spent long hours studying reference books. Models of civilian figures, on the other hand, are usually 54-mm replicas of Victorians or Edwardians, and are bound by no such rules or regulations. Certainly their dress must, again, faithfully represent the originals, but because there is rarely any uniformity about civilian clothes you are able to use your imagination.

The figures in the range I produced included Fagin, a street urchin, a ragged match girl, a golfer in plus-fours, a man in an old-fashioned bathing costume and a chimney sweep. You will have your own favourites, and for inspiration will turn to worn

A group of civilian figures. The match girl on the left is a white metal casting. The others are original master figures, all of which have been made by using Milliput to convert other figures

albums containing sepia prints of your own ancestors, and excellent reference books that will fascinate you as you read about trades and professions that have disappeared with the passing of time.

I came across a copy of *Mayhew's London*, which is described as 'the classic account of London street life and characters in the time of Charles Dickens and Queen Victoria'. To turn its pages is to step back in time to a period that, for the ordinary working class person, was one of squalor and unceasing hard work. You will find costermongers, London flower girls, sheeps'-trotter women, running patterers, music 'duffers', sewer hunters and mudlarks, and learn that the average London household consumed 11 tons of coal a year. A street comb seller could earn perhaps nine shillings a week (45 new pence), and lodgings, of a kind, could be found for tuppence a night (one new penny).

If you are accustomed to producing soldiers from the more colourful periods of history you will find that civilians' figures are, by comparison, quite drab. The rags worn by Fagin and the Artful Dodger might once have been brightly hued, but repeated dragging through the filth of London's streets and a long succession of washes in boiling water laced with soda left them stained and faded. What remained were various shades of grey, brown and black, with tinges of brighter colour visible in folds and creases.

But it's in the sheer variety of the clothing worn in those days that the interest lies. You will depict street vendors dressed in a collarless shirt, waistcoat, ragged jacket and torn overcoat, each one visible because all that holds them together is a piece of coarse twine around the waist. The trousers may also be tied with string, just above the worn boots. And the hat perched atop ragged, unkempt hair might be anything from a cloth cap to a battered topper. Flower girls will wear voluminous petticoats under long dresses revealing high-laced boots. Their shoulders will be draped in a shawl, and the posies they are selling will be splashes of bright colour in a basket.

All of these figures can be freely modelled in Milliput, which is a familiar compound admirably suited to the rendering of folds in loose clothing. You will find that garments created in soft Milliput and worked on with modelling tools and a wet brush will take on the look of draped cloth, and when painted in gloss enamels these charming little figures will impress all who see them.

In addition, they will add variety to your catalogue, and attract customers who are unmoved by military figures but have an abiding interest in people.

Connoisseur Figures

If you have a successful business manufacturing toy soldiers, why move into the field of unpainted connoisseur figures? One main reason, really: the work involved is far less labour-intensive.

We've already looked at the various processes of designing, manufacturing and selling toy soldiers, and if you are a modeller enjoying your hobby but contemplating a business the aspect most likely to put you off is the thought of all the work involved. Everyone in business expects to work hard, but there is a vast difference between, say, the production of toy soldiers as we have been discussing it, and the production of Airfix plastic figures. The former we already know about; in the latter case there is just the casting (or injection moulding) and the figures that emerge are packed in boxes and sold. No involvement with outworkers. No painstaking final painting. No red boxes with carefully designed labels.

There is a way around this dependence on labour, even without attempting to make connoisseur figures, as we have already seen. Many toy soldier collectors like to paint the figures themselves, so there is a good market for unpainted castings – and you can even sell spare parts: heads, bodies, weapons.

If your toy soldier castings can be sold unpainted, this would seem to be another argument against the production of connoisseur figures. You'll be satisfied for a while, but then the business expert within you will say, Hang on, I'm selling these castings at *x* pounds each; all I've got to do is refine them and I can double my selling price. The artist inside you will agree and say, yes, that's right, and I like a challenge: I want to know if I'm good enough to make it in the world of connoissseur military figures.

In fact, you almost certainly are. If your toy soldiers are already correctly proportioned and you are able to create interesting poses, then all that's required is to sharpen the detail. You may have been a little heavy handed, knowing that toy soldiers are expected to be crude. Boots will look too heavy, the representation of material at cuffs and jacket hems will be too thick, muskets will look like broomsticks. When making a 54-mm connoisseur figure you must model *everything* to the correct scale – even the smallest buttons! Thin everything down. Sharpen edges. Make curved or flat surfaces absolutely smooth. Put in detail where previously it has been omitted. Show the dividing line between a boot's sole and upper. Show the laces. And on your 54-mm connoisseur figure's face, put tiny eyeballs between recognizable eyelids – because the collector who buys your figures will certainly want to paint them!

Larger Figures

Progress is inevitable, and as a modeller you will almost certainly next feel the urge to stretch yourself by creating figures in a different scale. Although there is a lot of activity in the market for 54-mm soldiers, if you are anything like me your interest will be drawn by much larger figures – 75 mm, 90 mm, 100 mm and 120 mm.

Once you do this you will feel the same freedom that you discovered when you diversified into civilian figures: modelling eyeballs on a 54-mm connoisseur figure requires a steady hand, and either eyes like a hawk or a good magnifying glass; after that, working on a 120-mm figure will feel like putting the detail on the Statue of Liberty!

Exactly the same criteria apply, only more so. Working in 120 mm there is nowhere to hide. Everything must be exactly right, and in the right place. Detail that in 54 mm – even 54-mm connoisseur – was just too small to be represented, will now need to be modelled with a sculptor's skill and the authenticity expected from a military historian.

But the rewards are well worth the effort. The labour involved finishes with the sculpting (you can even get specialist firms to make the moulds and cast in metal or resin), a perfectly formed and posed 120-mm figure is an impressive sight, and when painted in oils by a skilled specialist such figures will grace any room.

Conclusions We have indeed digressed somewhat from the main body of this book which was all about *Modelling Toy Soldiers*. Nevertheless I hope the brief look at the way you can progress has aroused your interest, whetted your appetite, and at the very least suggested other ways to exercise your modelling skills. No doubt by now you have already discovered that dipping into military reference books for uniform details is something like looking for information in an encyclopaedia: you get diverted, find yourself deeply involved in accounts of a stirring battle which itself leads to other armies, other campaigns – and so it goes on.

Most of all, I hope that the contents the title of this book led you to expect were all there, all helpful, and have enabled you to start from scratch and produce at the very least one painted toy soldier.

If it leads you into a successful business, you can be sure that I will looking for that new business name and that unique style in the pages of *Military Modelling* and in the glass showcases at Under Two Flags of London.

Appendix A:
A Brief History of Toy Soldiers

Military Modelling, for a lot of people, means 'toy soldiers'. Here in Britain, and all over the world, the man who is still a boy at heart parades his massed ranks of figures in expensive cabinets, often paying very high prices at auction for what might appear to be drab, poorly painted nursery rejects. But they have charm; they are popular; and over the past few years the value of rare sets has appreciated dramatically.

Model soldiers are no modern phenomenon, of course. Military figures were placed in Egyptian tombs to protect the departed pharaohs, and painted wooden figures representing Egyptian heavy infantry, discovered in the tomb of Prince Emsah, are over 4,000 years old. But these were usually large figures, made for a specific, very serious purpose. The true 'toy' soldiers were originally inexpensive figures made to be played with, broken and replaced; and a recognized starting-point in their history would be Germany, in the middle of the eighteenth century.

Johann Gottfried Hilpert, who began his working life making kitchen utensils with his father, Andreas, moved to Nuremberg when he was eighteen and eventually qualified as a master tinsmith. By the year 1770 his workshop was producing a variety of farm and wildlife figures, but by the end of that decade, in an area where tin mines were flourishing despite the effects of the Seven Years War, he had turned to manufacturing flat toy soldiers, or *Zinnfiguren*. He was the first commercial producer to be identified. This dynasty, consisting of Johann's son, Johann Wolfgang, and his younger brother, Johann Georg, produced exquisite flat figures depicting Frederick the Great's armies and others from France, Russia and Turkey. They were packed on straw in split-pine boxes, marked in varying ways – H, JH, JGH or HILPERT – and were between 50 and 60 mm in height. The firm finally closed in 1801, when Johann Gottfried died at the age of sixty-eight. His moulds were bought by Johann Ludwig Stahl, who remained in business for seventeen years, but unfortunately could not maintain the excellent standards set by Hilpert.

Flat toy soldiers continued to be made by a number of manufacturers, the employees working in atrocious conditions for very low pay, the painters often very young children.

But as yet there was no standard scale, and it was not until about 1848 that Ernst Heinrichsen introduced the size – 30 mm – that was to become known as the Nuremberg Scale. Popular with both manufacturers and their customers, it was quickly taken up by makers all over Germany. The tiny, flat figures were sold in vast quantities, mostly by weight – 330 figures weighing approximately 1 kg – and this standardization meant that collectors could now assemble massed armies using figures produced by any or all of the leading manufacturers. Not surprisingly Heinrichsen – whose figures were marked E.H. or E.HEINRICHSEN – had many years of success, and survived until after the Second World War.

The First World War did reduce the output of the toy soldier manufacturers, but the cessation of hostilities saw production gradually pick up again.

Not long after the founding of a German association of collectors in 1924, yet another manufacturer appeared on the scene, this time in the north German town of Kiel. This firm – Fabrik für Kultürische Zinnfiguren und Kultürbilder, GmbH Kiel – was later taken over by Aloys Ochel of Kiel and was destined to become the world's largest manufacturer of tin figures. They were produced to the standard Nuremberg scale, marked K – for Kiel and Kultur – and were sold, painted or unpainted, in cardboard boxes.

The first challenge to these flat German figures came from France. And although recorded history is vague, it seems that a Parisian maker called Lucotte produced the first commercial, full-round figure at about the time of the French Revolution, in 1789.

What is known for certain is that in the early part of the nineteenth century, Lucotte was taken over by three makers, Cuperly, Blondel and Gerbau. They, in their turn, were taken over, this time by Mignot; but their initials – CBG – can be seen to this day, and CBG Mignot is recognized as the oldest maker still in production, with a stock of between 15,000 and 20,000 wonderful old moulds of mostly 54-mm figures.

Germany, too, did produce its share of fully rounded figures, and the firm founded by Georg Heyde introduced figures which were a natural progression from the semi-round figures already produced by such makers as Ammon, Haffner and Heinrichsen. Heyde produced soldiers from about 1870 to 1945, and although his figures were often clumsy, poorly and even wrongly dressed, and made with almost no regard for scale, the variety of poses has rarely been matched. So popular were his figures that they were frequently copied, notably by the McLoughlin Brothers of New York, the St Louis Soldier Company and by the Japanese.

In London, in 1893, a mounted model of the Life Guards appeared on the toy soldier scene. Carrying a thin strip of tin for a sword, extraordinarily light in weight, the figure met with little success until Gamage's of Holborn saw the potential in this new, revolutionary model. Albert Gamage ordered a batch of the figures in their crimson boxes, they were a sell-out, and the rest, as they say, is history.

The figure was, of course, No. 1 in the catalogue of soldiers to be produced by the British firm founded by William Britain, whose economical, hollow-cast technique took the toy soldier world by storm.

Over the years Britain's were to become undisputed leaders of the worldwide toy soldier industry. Always ready to produce new figures as military campaigns and wars flared up and died, able also to adapt to world economic and political change – during the First World War they produced millions of shrapnel balls, and metal tokens to be spent in military canteens – their familiar red boxes and delightful hand-painted contents were hoarded by children, royalty and avid collectors everywhere, until the production of lead soldiers ceased in 1967.

The list of toy soldier products is quite staggering, almost every industrialized nation having its quota.

During the inter-war years in the United States, the Barclay Manufacturing Company of West Hoboken, New Jersey, produced 'dimestore' soldiers known respectively and affectionately as Short Stride, Long Stride and Pod Foot. Manoil of New York was another prolific producer.

Otto and Max Hausser began making composition soldiers in 1904 in Ludwigsberg, southern Germany, using the trade name Elastolin. Manufactured from a material composed of sawdust, glue, kaolin and linseed oil the figures, though crude, proved extremely popular. With encouragement from Adolf Hitler, the firm prospered even during the years of the Second World War, and unlike their competitors, Lineol, who were wiped out, they have continued producing in a modified plastic form to this day.

The Spanish toy soldier industry was started in Barcelona in 1828 when Carlos Ortelli, an Italian, began producing flat figures. Full- round solid figures appeared at the beginning of the twentieth century, notably from the workshops of Eulogio Gonzalez and Baldomero Casanellas.

In Great Britain in the 1990s tin-alloy toy soldiers are still produced, but no longer are they intended for children. Expense and modern health regulations have meant that these 'new old toy soldiers' are manufactured to supply the very active collectors' market. In a variety of styles and qualities, ranging from crude stick figures to finely detailed miniatures, a host of craft-orientated firms both small and large is supplying collectors all over the world. Notable specialist names in this field are Dorset Soldiers, Ducal, Great Britain and The Empire Toy Soldiers, Langley Models, Trophy Miniatures of Wales, Steadfast and Tradition, while many other non-specialist firms produce toy soldiers as part of a larger marketing strategy.

In a field where apparent simplicity of design hides a wealth of skill and historical knowledge, and where business acumen is, as always, vital for survival, new firms come and go almost overnight. One typical survivor is Len Taylor of Trophy Miniatures, who began his business from a hobby in 1976 and today exports to many overseas dealers and individual collectors.

Trophy, perhaps, epitomizes this 'skilful simplicity', and although the figures are solid, this South Wales firm uses working methods which are not too far removed from those of the legendary Britain's. Masters are produced by skilled pattern-makers, inter-moulds of silicone rubber are manufactured, and then the final, hot-vulcanised rubber mould. The shiny castings produced in Trophy's workshops are then cleaned, assembled and delivered to a small army of outworkers who do much of the bulk-painting. Final touches are added by Trophy's own skilled painters. It's a system that works well and, with modifications, is used by most of the firms producing today's 'new old toy soldiers'.

In recent years nostalgia, which used to connote 'homesickness', has taken on a new meaning, and is now recognized as describing that condition where people look back with affection on days gone by. The 'new old toy soldiers' appeared on the scene partly as a result of this new wave of sentimentality, and have since prospered as collectible items in their own right.

But who do they go to, these beautiful, gloss-painted figures in their bright red boxes? And who are the people who, to this day, continue to collect the ragged survivors of the toy soldier armies created by those magnificent early craftsmen? In the past the collectors were royalty, simply because they were the only ones who could afford it. Louis XIII of France owned one of the most valuable collections, and owed its existence to his mother on whose instructions it was made from fine silver. The collection was inherited by Louis XIV who added to it and was then forced to sell it to fund his wars.

King Ferdinand II of Naples also had a fine collection, as did Napoleon III's heir, the Prince Imperial. In recent times, perhaps the world's largest and certainly the most famous assembly of toy soldiers was the Forbes collection, which was put on display in Tangier's Palais Mendoub in the early 1970s and grew from relatively small beginnings to a million-dollar display. But while there will always be individuals or corporations such as these, able to utilize their vast wealth to amass very large collections, the picture of the average collector, if one exists, is very different indeed.

Many youngsters who grew up during the heyday of the Britain's dynasty regularly received those distinctive red boxes, either on birthdays or at Christmas, and the seeds sown in childhood tended to germinate a lot later in life.

After years of neglect the old toys would be rescued from cupboards, attics and battered trunks at the back of box rooms, dusted off and looked at afresh. These embryo collections developed, and still develop, in very individual ways, in most cases with little thought for potential value. Many collectors simply add figures similar to those resurrected childhood toys, which means concentrating on soldiers from the age of Victoria and the colourful campaigns embarked on by 'the Widow at Windsor's' troops in her colonies. Often, the collector will specialize in the soldiers produced by William Britain.

Others start with no set plan, and continue that way; they acquire scruffy figures from jumble or car-boot sales, from relatives and from the fast-disappearing junk shops; they attend auctions and bid when the price is right, and finish up with a collection which, while having no recognizable theme, does have astonishing variety.

Still others eschew the old figures altogether and concentrate on those from the new manufacturers, safe in the knowledge that new issues are regularly released (and will naturally be in pristine condition) and that a good collection can be built up without too much expense.

In 1828 Captain William Siborne's model of the Battle of

Waterloo went on display in London, featuring some 190,000 tiny, 13-mm figures. The Forbes collection has already been mentioned, as have those of the early French and Italian monarchs. Mickey's House of Soldiers in Sunnyvale, California, is reputed to have on display 250,000 soldiers, from all the producing countries. All such displays have always been extremely popular – but what is their attraction?

Shamus Wade of Nostalgia – a pioneering 'new old toy soldier' firm that produced some of the very first of that new wave, and always destroyed the moulds after the initial run of castings – once quoted a fellow collector's views on the subject. 'The most important thing about a soldier,' this colleague remarked, 'is that he is a member of a group.' He might have added that the 'toy' soldier also has an intrinsic charm perhaps not present in any other military miniatures.

The famous makers of German flat figures knew this when the Nuremberg standard was created and the tiny figures sold in their thousands. Today anyone who sees massed ranks of toy soldiers on display, anywhere, is immediately struck by the same feeling. It's almost as if the individual figures are unimportant; the overall effect is paramount, and in this respect the toy soldier, from the crudest to the most exquisite, from those finely engraved 30-mm flats to the latest 54-mm full-round figures, stands supreme.

Previously published, in a slightly different form, in *Military Modelling*, June and July 1990.

Appendix B:
Selected Reference Books

Ascoli, David, *A Companion to the British Army* (Harrap, 1983)

Blair, Claude, *European Armour* (Batsford, 1958)

Cassin-Scott, Jack, *Model Soldiers* (Batsford, 1990)

Dixey, Graham, *Military Modelling: The Art of the Model Soldier* (Argus 1988)

Ehrlich & Kurtz, *The Art of the Toy Soldier* (New Cavendish, 1987)

Featherstone, Donald, *Better Military Modelling* (Kaye & Ward, 1977)

Goodenough, Simon, *Military Miniatures* (Orbis Publishing, 1977)

Johnson, Peter, *Toy Armies* (Batsford, 1981)

Jones, Ken, *The Military Modeller's Compendium* (Argus, 1992)

Lawford, James, *The Cavalry* (Samson Low, 1976)

Mollo, John & McGregor, Malcolm, *Uniforms of the American Revolution* (Blandford Press, 1975)

Myatt, Frederick, *The British Infantry, 1660–1945* (Blandford, 1983)

Opie, James, *Toy Soldiers* (Shire Publications, 1983)

Ruddle, John, *Collectors' Guide to Britains Model Soldiers* (Model and Allied Publications, 1980)

Taylor, Arthur, *Discovering Model Soldiers* (Shire Publications, 1972)

Translated from the Italian by Massimo Alberini, *Model Soldiers* (Orbis Publishing, 1972)
Various authors, *Men at Arms Series* (Osprey)

Appendix C:
Equipment and Material Suppliers

Casting Resins and Silicone Rubbers

Alec Tiranti Ltd,
70 High Street,
Theale,
Reading,
Berkshire RG7 5AR
  Tel: 01734 302 775
  Fax: 01734 323 487

Island Scientific (Medina Art Castings Ltd)
Unit 4,
Ventnor Industrial Estate,
Station Road,
Ventnor
Isle of Wight PO38 1DX
  Tel: 01983 855 822
  Fax: 01983 852 146

Display Cases, Domes and Bases

Trireme,
7 Gullin Drive,
Prestwick,
Ayrshire,
Scotland KA9 2TL
  Tel: 01292 678 070

SAS Showcases Ltd,
24 Chapel Hill,
Ropsley,
Grantham,
Lincolnshire NG33 4BP
  Tel/Fax: 01476 585 015

Craft Supplies,
Millers Dale,
Buxton,
Derbyshire SK17 8SN
  Tel: 01298 871 636

The Glass Dome Co.,
62 Priory Road,
Tonbridge,
Kent TN9 2BL
  Tel: 01732 367 181
  Fax: 01732 360 830

Wiremill Design,
Four Crosses,
Wiremill Lane,
Newchapel,
Lingfield,
Surrey RH7 6HJ
  Tel: 01342 834 918

R.A. Cannons,
The Old Stores,
Kingscott,
St Giles in the Wood,
Torrington,
Devon EX38 7JW
  Tel: 01805 623 816

Elisena sri,
Via I.Garbini, 73,
01100 Viterbo,
Italy
  Tel: (39) 761 251119
Fax: (39) 761 250975

Magazines and other Publications

Military Modelling,
Nexus House,
Boundary Way,
Hemel Hempstead,
Hertfordshire HP2 7ST
  Tel: 01442 66551

Regiment,
Nexus House,
Boundary Way,
Hemel Hempstead,
Hertfordshire HP2 7ST
  Tel: 01442 66551

The Old Toy Soldier,
209 North Lombard,
Oak Park,
Illinois 60302-2503
USA

Military Bookshops

History Bookshop,
2 Broadway
Friern Barnet Road
London N11 3DU
  Tel/Fax 0181 368 8568

Chelifer Books,
Curthwaite,
Carlisle,
Cumbria CA7 8BE
  Tel/Fax: 01228 711 388

Military Services,
87 Ellacombe Road,
Longwell Green,
Bristol,
Avon BS15 6BP
  Tel: 0117 324 085

Picton Publishing,
Chippenham,
Wiltshire SN15 2NS

Keegan's Bookshop,
Merchant's Place,
Friar Street,
Reading,
Berkshire RG1 1DT
  Tel: 01734 587 253

Connoisseur Military Books,
11a Devonshire Road,
Chiswick,
London W4 2EU
  Tel: 0181 742 0022

The Collector,
36 The Colonnade,
Piece Hall,
Halifax,
W. Yorkshire HX1 1RS
    Tel: 01422 363 895

Hersant's Military Books,
17 The Drive,
High Barnet,
Hertfordshire EN5 4JG
    Tel/Fax: 0181 440 6816

Military and Aviation Book
Society,
Swindon,
Wiltshire SN3 4BR

Motor Books
33–36 St Martin's Court,
Charing Cross Road,
London WC2N 4AL
    Tel: 0171 836 6728/5376/
        3800
    Fax: 0171 497 2539

Napoleon's Military Bookshop,
353 Flinders Lane,
Melbourne 3000,
Australia
    Tel: (03) 9629 3047

Napoleon's Military Bookshop,
1 North Quay,
Brisbane 4000,
Australia
    Tel:/Fax: (07) 229 1903

Napoleon's Military Bookshop,
336 Pitt Street,
Sydney 2000,
Australia
    Tel: (02) 264 7560

Miscellaneous Tools and Materials

Optum Hobby Aids,
P.O. Box 262,
Haywards Heath,
West Sussex RH16 3FR
    Tel: 01444 416 795
    Fax: 01444 458 606

Alec Tiranti Ltd,
70 High Street,
Theale,
Reading,
Berkshire RG7 5AR
    Tel: 01734 302 775
    Fax: 01734 323 487

David Proops Sales,
21 Masons Avenue,
Wealdstone,
Harrow,
Middlesex HA3 5AH
    Tel: 0181 861 5258
    Fax: 0181 861 5404

Model Shops and Dealers

Battlefield,
50 Clissold Parade,
Campsie,
Sydney
New South Wales, 2194
Australia
    Tel: (02) 718 2423
    Fax: (02) 718 3847

Warlords Hobby Shop,
25 Derrick Street,
Lalor,
Victoria 3075,
Australia
    Tel: (03) 9465 7587

Mary's Miniatures,
788 Reynold's Drive,
Kincardine,
Ontario N2Z 3A5
Canada
  Tel: (519) 396 4184
  Fax: (519) 396 9258

Classic Toys,
(in Greenwich Village),
218 Sullivan Street,
New York,
NY 10012
USA
  Tel: (212) 674 4434

Under Two Flags,
Military Antiquarians,
4 St Christophers Place,
Wigmore Street,
London W1M 5HB
  Tel: 0171 935 6934

Cowin Enterprises,
New York

Dutkins,
Philadelphia

Mickey's House of Soldiers,
California

Rubber Moulding Discs (for Vulcanizing)

Coker Bros Ltd,
Unit 11,
Upper Brents Industrial
  Estate,
Faversham,
Kent ME13 7DZ
  Tel: 01795 535 008
  Fax: 01795 532 146

Whitemetal Casting Alloys

Mountstar Metal Corporation
  Ltd,
Rail Works,
Railway Sidings,
Biggleswade,
Bedfordshire SG18 8BD
  Tel: 01767 318 444
  Fax: 01767 317 764

Geo. W. Neale Ltd,
Victoria Road,
London NW10 6NG
  Tel: 0181 965 1336

Fry's Metals Ltd,
Tandem House,
Marlowe Way,
Croydon,
Surrey CR0 4XS
  Tel: 0181 665 6666
  Fax: 0181 665 6196

Carn Metals Ltd,
2c Trewellard Industrial
  Estate,
Pendeen,
Penzance,
Cornwall TR19 7TF
  Tel:/Fax: 01736 787 343

Miscellaneous Services

Metal and Resin Casting

Resin 8,
22 Peregrine Close,
Winshill,
Burton upon Trent,
Staffordshire DE15 0EB
  Tel:/Fax: 01283 537104